Physical Characteristics of the Leonberger

(from the Fédération Cynologique Internationale breed standard)

Back: Firm, straight, broad.

Croup: Broad, relatively long, gently rounded.

Tail: Very well furnished; while standing, it hangs down straight.

Hindquarters: Pelvis: Slanting. Upper thigh: Rather long, slanting, strongly muscled. Upper and lower thigh form a distinct angle. Hocks: Strong, distinct angle between lower thigh and rear pastern. Hind feet: Standing straight, only slightly longish. Toes arched, pads black.

Underline and belly: Only slightly tucked up.

Color: Lion yellow, red, reddish brown, also sandy (pale yellow, cream colored) and all combinations in between, always with a black mask.

Hair: Medium soft to coarse, profusely long, close fitting, never parted, with the shape of the whole body visible despite the thick undercoat.

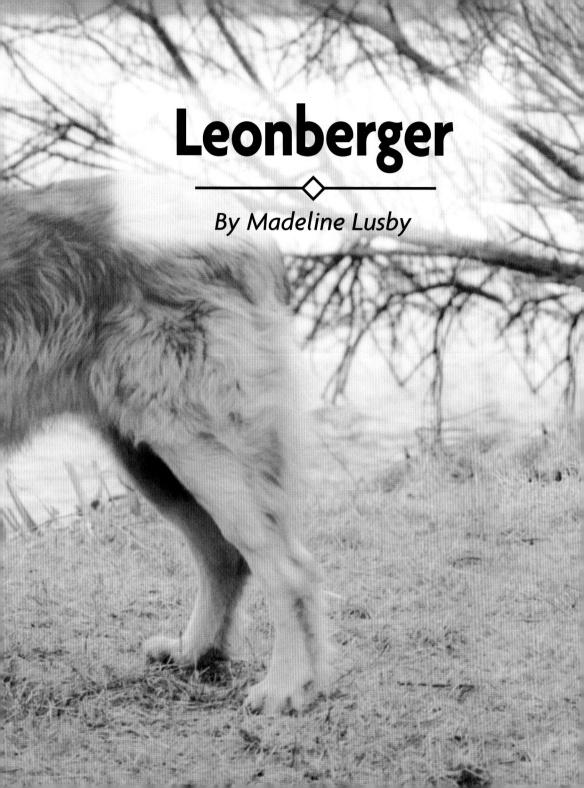

Leonberger

◇

By Madeline Lusby

Contents

9   History of the Leonberger

Meet the "lion of a breed" hailing from Leonberg, Germany and trace the beginnings of this multi-talented all-terrain working dog. Used for a variety of tasks requiring a broad range of skills, the Leo has quite an impressive résumé! Learn of the breed's brushes with royalty, meet the important people and dogs in the breed's establishment and follow the Leonberger's spread to regions outside its homeland.

19   Characteristics of the Leonberger

The Leo is truly one of a kind in personality and requires an equally special owner... are you right for the Leonberger? Discuss what it takes to own such a large, unique dog and read owners' accounts of their Leos' endearing quirks, sense of humor and uncanny intelligence. You, too, may become addicted to the Leonberger.

30   Breed Standard for the Leonberger

Learn the requirements of a well-bred Leonberger by studying the description of the breed as set forth in the Fédération Cynologique Internationale's breed standard. Both show dogs and pets must possess key characteristics as outlined in the breed standard.

38   Your Puppy Leonberger

Find out about how to locate a well-bred Leonberger puppy. Discover which questions to ask the breeder and what to expect when visiting the litter. Prepare for your puppy-accessory shopping spree. Also discussed are home safety, the first trip to the vet, socialization and solving basic puppy problems.

66   Proper Care of Your Leonberger

Cover the specifics of taking care of your Leonberger every day: feeding; grooming, including coat care, ears, eyes, nails and bathing; and exercise needs for your dog. Also discussed are dog ID, safe travel and boarding.

Training Your Leonberger   84

Begin with the basics of training the puppy and adult dog. Learn the principles of house-training the Leonberger, including the use of crates and basic scent instincts. Get started by introducing the pup to his collar and leash and progress to the basic commands. Find out about obedience classes and other activities.

Healthcare of Your Leonberger   111

By Lowell Ackerman DVM, DACVD
Become your dog's healthcare advocate and a well-educated canine keeper. Select a skilled and able veterinarian. Discuss pet insurance, vaccinations and infectious diseases, breed specific problems, the neuter/spay decision and a sensible, effective plan for parasite control, including fleas, ticks and worms.

Showing Your Leonberger   142

Step into the center ring and find out about the world of conformation showing for rare-breed dogs in the US. Here's how to get started in shows, how they are organized and what's required for your dog to become a champion. Take a leap into other areas of the dog sport and also meet the FCI, the "world kennel club."

Index 156

KENNEL CLUB BOOKS: **LEONBERGER**
ISBN: 1-59378-314-0

Copyright © 2005 • Kennel Club Books, LLC
308 Main Street, Allenhurst, NJ 07711 USA
Cover Design Patented: US 6,435,559 B2 • Printed in South Korea

Photography by:

Paulette Braun, T.J. Calhoun, Alan and Sandy Carey, Carolina Biological Supply, David Dalton, Isabelle Français, Lynette Hodge, Carol Ann Johnson, Bill Jonas, Dr. Dennis Kunkel, Madeline Lusby, Tam C. Nguyen, Phototake, Jean Claude Revy, Michael Trafford and Alice van Kempen.

Illustrations by Reneé Low and Patricia Peters.

The publisher wishes to thank John Feehan, Jane Guntripp, Lynette Hodge/Stormchaser Leonbergers, Tamaryn Hodge, Sheena & Larry Hooper, Sabine Klippel, Andrea & Dr. Helmut Kraus, Madeline Lusby/Shermayne Leonbergers, Bonnie Meldrum, F. Parry, Mathias Schroeder, Edith Steffen, Fran Williams, Martin Woetz and the rest of the owners of the dogs featured in this book.

A true "lion of a breed," Leonbergers Skye and Saffy pose against a mountainous vista befitting of their heritage.

HISTORY OF THE

LEONBERGER

The Leonberger has been described as a "man-made dog" and, as with many breeds today, is the result of crossing two or more breeds. The origins of the Leonberger go back to the 19th century. Leonbergers may have been in existence long before that, but stories tell of a man named Heinrich Essig, who was and still is considered to be the "father" of the breed. Essig was the mayor of the German city of Leonberg. He created his own ideal dog—the lion-like gentle giant—which he named after the town and saw it as a tribute to the lion that was part of the town's crest.

Essig's methods would appal the modern breeder—several breeds were housed in his commercial kennels and he sold 200–300 dogs a year. His estate must have resembled a menagerie with ducks, chickens, turkeys, pigeons, deer and foxes. His preference was for large dogs, and records show that he kept St. Bernards, Great Danes, Newfoundlands and Great Pyrenees in his kennels. His dream was to produce a handsome "lion of a dog" with a thick tawny golden coat, a dog that would be courageous and

Herr Essig, the father of the Leonberger, favored large breeds; the Great Dane was among the breeds he kept in his kennels.

loyal to his master. He experimented with the dogs in his kennels and mated a Landseer Newfoundland bitch to a large long-coated St. Bernard dog, which he had acquired from the monks at the Grand St. Bernhard hospice in Switzerland. This mating resulted in black and white offspring with pleasant temperaments.

After recrossing them for four generations, he then introduced a mountain dog and another St. Bernard male from the same hospice, which he exchanged for two of his puppies. The monks at the St. Bernhard hospice found Essig's dogs to be equal to their St. Bernards in every respect. The result of the mountain dog/St. Bernard mating was a predominantly white dog with a black or gray head. The mayor felt that more work was needed, so he introduced the Great Pyrenees to the mix and, in 1846, produced

The St. Bernard was one of the original breeds used to produce the Leonberger.

the dog of his dreams. It wasn't until some years later that the red-coated dogs we see today began to appear.

When the breed was officially introduced to the public at the Munich Oktoberfest some years later, its noble appearance made it an instant success. The beautiful gentle dog was sought after by royalty, and its fame spread throughout Europe. As well as being a very suitable family pet, it was also valued for its willingness to work on land and in water.

There were people at that time who were very critical of Essig's work. They felt that the Leonberger would hinder the development of the St. Bernard, as it was so often mistaken for the

PURE-BRED PURPOSE
Given the vast range of the world's 400 or so pure breeds of dog, it's fair to say that domestic dogs are the most versatile animal in the kingdom. From the tiny 1-pound lap dog to the 200-pound guard dog, dogs have adapted to every need and whim of their human masters. Humans have selectively bred dogs to alter physical attributes like size, color, leg length, mass and skull diameter in order to suit our own needs and fancies. Dogs serve humans not only as companions and guardians but also as hunters, exterminators, shepherds, rescuers, messengers, warriors, babysitters and more!

The addition of the Great Pyrenees into the breeding program resulted in success for Herr Essig's attempts in producing the Leo.

The Leo is no stranger to mountainous terrain and snowy climes, and still performs work in such regions today.

St. Bernard. However, the Leonberger became extremely fashionable and was sold to many courts across Europe for vast amounts of money.

When Essig died in 1889, the popularity of the Leonberger dwindled. A small number of enthusiasts kept the breed going and, in 1895, the International Leonberger Club was founded in Stuttgart. As years passed, other clubs were established: Klub für Leonberger Hunde in 1901 in Apolda; the Leonberger Club of Heidelberg in 1908; and the Leonberger (Hunde) Club in 1922 in Leonberg.

The Leonberger suffered during both World Wars and, after World War II, there were fewer than 300 Leonbergers left in Germany in 1945. The harsh post-war conditions were not conducive to restoring old or starting new breeding programs. Fortunately, the breed eventually recovered from near-extinction and, in 1948, the Deutscher Klub für Leonberger Hunde e.V. was founded in Leonberg. Its founding members, the first president Hans Weigelschmidt, Albert Kienzle and Otto Lehmann, were responsible for establishing the breed as we know it today. During the 1950s, the city of Leonberg took the club under its guardianship and recognized the Leonberger as its mascot. The Deutscher Klub thrives today and is the center for many Leonberger activities. Since 1946, the number of Leonbergers has increased dramatically. During the 1960s, they were bred profusely all over Europe and today approximately 1,000 are registered there each year.

In 1975, the Internationale Union für Leonberger Hunde was formed, its seat being in Leonberg. Each year, representatives from breed clubs all over the world meet to discuss the future of the Leonberger. In 1996, the 150-year celebration for the Leonberger was held in Leonberg, including a

SEARCH AND RESCUE

In some parts of Europe, Leonbergers are used in the mountainous regions for search and rescue, the same tasks for which St. Bernards have been used for generations.

A Landseer Newfoundland (shown here) was mated to a St. Bernard in the initial crosses used to create the Leonberger.

grand dinner held for Leo enthusiasts from all over the world, with some of the best dogs being presented to the audience. The breed show was held on the club's grounds the following day. Approximately 300 dogs had entered the show and, at the end of the day, Best in Show was awarded to a German bitch named Kiseirdi Nora. The breed continues to be strong in its homeland, with the Leo population well over 5,000.

EARLY BREED HISTORY

According to Austrian historical findings taken from journals, letters and old paintings, the Leonberger had been in existence approximately 300 years before Herr Essig's idea of breeding a lion-like dog was ever realized. The late Professor von Schulmuth researched various family journals and discovered that the breed was

Carting was once the Leo's occupation, but now he's more likely to be seen carting in exhibitions or giving a ride to a young pal.

WAR HERO
During the two World Wars, Leonbergers were used to pull the ammunition carts, a service to the breed's country that sadly resulted in the Leo's near-destruction.

known as early as 1585, and probably even earlier. The family of Prince Metternich lived near Wolfberg and their private records dated 1601 state that a Leonberger-type dog was kept on the estate to ward off sheep and cattle thieves.

Among the other people recorded as having kept Leonbergers were the Empress Elizabeth of Austria, who kept seven dogs. (A statue of her with two of her dogs can be seen in the Volksgarten in Vienna.) King Umberto of Italy loved them, the Emperor Maximilian was constantly accompanied by his dog, and the Mikado of Japan kept them at his palaces. In the 16th century, the imperial family of Austria had kennels of Leonberger-type dogs, from which the Metternich family received their dogs.

During the 1800s, Leonbergers were frequently seen being used, singly or in pairs, pulling carts around Württemberg, Bavaria and Austrian villages, although this is now only seldom seen except in the most remote of villages.

After a trip to Austria, Marie Antoinette brought some dogs back with her. This ties in with further information from Mademoiselle de Gineste, of Courivause, Marne, France, whose ancestor, the Marquis de Pluival, was a page at the court of Marie Antoinette. He liked these dogs so much that the queen presented him with some, which he took to his home. The Gineste family can trace some of their dogs back to the Marquis's first dogs.

In recent years, the experts have put forward less colorful theories of how the Leonberger developed. During the 19th century and probably earlier, there were many Alpine dogs in the regions of the Black Forest. They would come down from the hills with their owners to the market towns, and it has been suggested that on these occasions they may have been crossed with the long-coated, heavy-boned shepherds from the southern regions of Germany. This would account for the unique coloration of the Leonberger, as it would be genetically impossible to attain the breed's coloring from the dogs that Heinrich Essig claims to have used.

THE LEONBERGER IN THE UNITED STATES

In the early 1980s, the Leonberger was barely in existence in the United States. There were 17 known dogs up until 1985. Then Mary and Reiner Decher's bitch, Fiona, gave birth to 14 puppies, just about doubling the population! Selling puppies of an unknown breed was a difficult task at that time, and many of the pups had to be given away.

That same year, Reiner Decher instigated a meeting of Leonberger breeders and owners. Along with Reiner and Mary Decher, fanciers Sylvia and Manfred Kaufmann, Yves Parent, Waltraud Zieher, Kerry Campbell, Melanie Brown and Brian Peters met in Denver, Colorado to establish the Leonberger Club of America (LCA). At the same time, the

CANIS LUPUS

"Grandma, what big teeth you have!" The gray wolf, a familiar figure in fairy tales and legends, has had its reputation tarnished and its population pummeled over the centuries. Yet it is the descendants of this much-feared creature to which we open our homes and hearts. Our beloved dog, *Canis domesticus*, derives directly from the gray wolf, a highly social canine that lives in elaborately structured packs. In the wild, the gray wolf can range from 60 to 175 pounds, standing between 25 and 40 inches in height.

A handsome Leo trio from the Netherlands.

club's Code of Ethics, Rules and Regulations and *Leo Letter* (the club's official publication) were established.

The next official meeting took place in Ontario, Canada at the club's first national specialty show. The founding members and others crowded into a small trailer and talked until the early morning hours, discussing their plans and goals for the club. Together they worked out the guidelines for their new club, which included electing officers and establishing plans and responsibilities. The club's aim was (and still is) to maintain the health and soundness of their beloved breed.

Nabilah-Nerahsha von Welland the Stormchaser ("Storm"), a top-winning bitch in Great Britain, pictured at two years of age.

Since that day, the Leonberger Club of America has gone from strength to strength. As a result of the ever-increasing popularity of the Leonberger breed, regional clubs sanctioned by the LCA were formed. These clubs, such as the Northwest Leonberger Club, the Rocky Mountain Leonberger Club, the Northern and Southern California Leonberger Clubs and many more, all organize their own specialty shows each year with the emphasis on having fun with their Leos. Dogs and owners travel all around the country to attend these functions, meeting with friends, showing their Leos and taking pleasure in the sight of so many Leonbergers gathered together in one place!

The Leonberger Club of America is the official registry for Leonbergers in the United States. The club is not affiliated with the American Kennel Club, as the breed is not AKC-recognized, but

the club is a member of the International Union für Leonberger Hunde (IULH). The IULH is the same club started in Leonberg in 1975; it now has member countries all over the world. The Fédération Cynologique Internationale (FCI) breed standard, which is set forth by the national breed club of Germany, the Deutscher Klub für Leonberger Hunde, is the standard to which

the LCA adheres, promoting careful breeding practices in accordance with the standard of the breed's homeland.

Two very impressive Leonberger kennels in the United States are the Kennel von Alpensee and the Kennel von Jagen. Both kennels have had substantial wins at many national shows. Alida Comtois and Susan Grosslight are both responsible breeders who spend time researching their potential studs and brood bitches in order to produce dogs of top quality. Thanks to dedicated breeders like these, and the efforts of all of the LCA's various committees, the future of the breed in this country is on a strong footing.

Int. Ch. Radjhivon Lowenkraft, a champion male from Belgium.

Int. Ch. Kiseirdi Nora, pictured with handler Sabine Klippel, was Best in Show at the 1996 German Club Show, marking the breed's 150-year celebration.

LEONBERGER CLUB OF AMERICA

The LCA can be found online at www.leonbergerclubofamerica.com. This site is very comprehensive, with information about the breed and the club itself and offering many resources for breeders, owners and fanciers as well as newcomers to the breed.

The guardian of the yard! Protective instinct is at the fore of the Leonberger's temperament, as he is tremendously loyal to his family and watches over the home and property.

CHARACTERISTICS OF THE

LEONBERGER

ALL ABOUT THE LEO

The typical Leonberger is faithful, intelligent, amenable, web-footed and a very protective. However, dogs, like humans, can have very definite personalities. Leonbergers are described as being equable and, in general, they are, but they can be very excitable dogs, quite often being over-the-top with their greetings. They are also very affable and seek attention from anyone close at hand. Their affection is unlimited, and they always give it generously. The following explanations are just a few examples in an attempt to describe our wonderful breed.

The expression "Gentle Giant" is true, but only if the dog has been carefully bred for tempera-ment and not just looks. Most importantly, Leos must be well socialized and continually trained from eight weeks of age until they reach maturity, which takes at least until two to three years of age. In general, Leonbergers are lively, fun-loving dogs, totally devoted to and protective of their human families, particularly the younger members. Leonbergers that are aggressive toward people,

particularly children, do *not* represent the desired and typical temperament of the breed. The typical Leo is an easy dog to live with, asking for no more than a bowl of food, water, regular exercise and his owners' companionship. However, the Leo is not a recommended breed for the first-time dog owner, because, although they look like fluffy teddy bears when puppies, they grow into very large and exceedingly strong "bears" in only a matter of a few months.

There are several characteris-tics that differ between dogs and bitches, some of which become noticeable at certain times in their lives, which is why it is important to thoroughly understand the breed before deciding to buy a puppy. When talking to Leonberger owners, it is fairly common to find that each person has a personal preference as to whether it is easier to live with a dog or a bitch.

The males have two stages in their early lives during which hormones are stronger incentives than their owners' pleas and frantic waving of biscuits (this is

"Lap dog" is not the first term that comes to mind when describing the Leonberger...but just try to convince the Leo otherwise!

youngsters; in fact, other than the normal naughty puppy behavior, they are perhaps easier than their male counterparts. They tend to have their first season (heat cycle) at around 12 months and can come into season as often as every 4 months, but every 6 months is more common. As the bitch matures and becomes of breeding age, she can be prone to behavioral changes from anywhere up to three weeks before her season starts and then during her three-week cycle.

It is not uncommon for the bitch to change from a lovable family pet to a touchy dog with an attitude of "don't you come

when all of that early training becomes invaluable). Of course, this will differ from dog to dog, but generally these periods occur at approximately 6–9 months of age, then again between 14–18 months of age. At these times, the male Leo seems to forget all of his previous training and begins to assert himself within his pack (which includes all two-legged members of the household!).

A male, as an adult, can become aggressive toward others of his own sex, particularly when he has been used at stud. Although it might seem that males are nothing but trouble, with all that testosterone rushing through their bodies, they generally grow into much more sensitive pets and appreciate all the love and attention lavished upon them. (If the truth be known, they can become "mama's boys.")

Bitches tend to have fewer stages of disruptive behavior as

HEART-HEALTHY

In this modern age of ever-improving cardio-care, no doctor or scientist can dispute the advantages of owning a dog to lower a person's risk of heart disease. Studies have proven that petting a dog, walking a dog and grooming a dog all show positive results toward lowering your blood pressure. The simple routine of exercising your dog—going outside with the dog and walking, jogging or playing catch—is heart-healthy in and of itself. If you are normally less active than your physician thinks you should be, adopting a dog may be a smart option to improve your own quality of life as well as that of another creature.

DOG DETECTIVE

Leonbergers have an extremely keen sense of smell. One day a Leonberger named Bruno was out walking with his owner alongside a riverbank. He became intensely interested in a particular part of the riverbank and, upon close inspection, the owner discovered the dog had found the body of a man. Prior to this, the police had made intense searches of the river and surrounding areas with tracking dogs, but had never found the body.

anywhere near me" when she has been mated, quite often as early as within 24 hours of the breeding.

Later on in her pregnancy, a bitch appears to become more contented with life and does not relish the thought of taking part in any rough behavior, especially not tolerating it from other dogs. For the family pet, not to be used for breeding or showing, neutering/spaying can eliminate most sex-related behavior issues as well as offering important health benefits to both sexes.

The Leonberger who has been brought up in a family environment is instinctively very protective toward the children of the household. The Leo can have a real rapport with younger members of the family; this is true of both dogs and bitches. Of

Leos love their "people" and aren't afraid to show it. Khan gives mom Lyn Hodge a kiss, while his pups squeeze in for a cuddle.

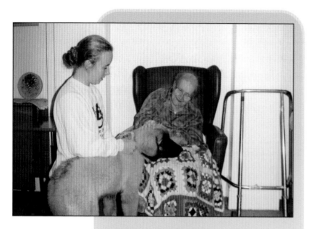

DELTA SOCIETY

The human-animal bond propels the work of the Delta Society, striving to improve the lives of people and animals. The Pet Partners Program proves that the lives of people and dogs are inextricably linked. The Pet Partners Program, a national registry, trains and screens volunteers for pet therapy in hospices, nursing homes, schools and rehabilitation centers. Dog-and-handler teams of Pet Partners volunteer in all 50 states, with nearly 7,000 teams making visits annually. About 900,000 patients, residents and students receive assistance each year. If you and your dog are interested in becoming Pet Partners, visit the Delta Society online at www.deltasociety.org.

course, the children should always treat the family dog gently and with respect, and their interactions should be supervised.

A young male Leo that lived with a large family was one day allowed into the bathroom to watch the babies being bathed. When the children were placed in the water, he panicked and tried to pull them out. His attempts to "rescue" them were thwarted by his owner, so he frantically tried to scoop the water out of the bath with his paws. This example shows just how devoted and protective Leonbergers can be of their families, and how they can use their intelligence to figure problems out. Unable to accomplish a task in a certain way, the Leo "thinks" of other methods to reach the same goal.

The Leonberger enjoys being an integral part of the family. When left alone for even the shortest time period, his greeting can be most enthusiastic, nearly knocking over even the strongest person. A typical greeting can range from a wagging tail with lots of wet kisses to jumping up to look you in the eye, while wriggling his entire body, and with plenty of "doggy chat," telling you how much he has missed you. Visitors to your home could find this rather intimidating, and a Leonberger's greeting can be misunderstood by those who are new to the breed. This can be avoided by early training. Leos may grow out of this behavior, but not until maturity or older, even up to six or seven years of age.

When the family has settled

LEO HELPERS

Leonbergers can swim exceedingly well and are capable of performing the same tasks in water as the Newfoundland, e.g., pulling in a boat and saving a drowning person. Further, Leonbergers are now being used as guide dogs and assistance dogs, providing invaluable aid to their owners with special needs. Many Leos are certified therapy dogs, visiting the sick and elderly in hospitals and nursing homes.

into an evening of watching television, a Leonberger will expect to be part of this gathering. He will quite happily climb up on the sofa or, better still, will plant his bottom on your lap to watch the show with you. He may even attempt to persuade you to give in and let him have the armchair. As far as he is concerned, what is good enough for his family is good enough for him to share equally. He sees himself as a member of the family and wants his fair share of everything.

Some dogs can be quite aloof with people they do not know, keeping their distance while they assess the situation. An owner, while out walking with her dog in a quiet secluded place, was approached by an unruly and aggressive group of youths with the intention of wrongdoing. The dog seemed to grow in stature,

gave a meaningful warning growl and positioned himself between his owner and the youths. Due to the intimidating size and posturing of the dog, what could have been a nasty situation was averted. Minutes later, coming across a family with young children, the same dog stood quite still, allowing the children to cuddle and caress him while he enjoyed all the attention.

This is an intelligent breed, although perhaps not quite so eager to please and carry out

every command instantly as would a German Shepherd Dog or Border Collie. Some Leonbergers have excellent working qualities and, mixed with their love of human companionship, it is not surprising that Leonbergers are now working as guide dogs for the blind and as assistance dogs for the disabled. In some mountainous regions, Leonbergers are proving to be invaluable as search and rescue dogs, following in the pawprints of their St. Bernard ancestors.

For the Leonbergers that have

Bramble practices water work by "rescuing" his owner.

signs of a puppy's growth, the pup's progression through different uses of the water bowl tells part of the story. Initially the puppy will put his face under the water and blow bubbles, and then he will dig out the water with his paw. The next stage is when he only seems capable of drinking if one leg is in the bowl (which finishes up with his standing completely in the bowl while he "snorkels" and gives the impression of fishing). Even an adult Leonberger's idea of drinking water is that as much water as possible should be all over the floor and not in the bowl.

The Leonberger also loves the open air. It does not matter to him what the weather is like. In rain, sun, snow or howling winds, he likes the door open for easy access to both home and yard (securely fenced, of course). He thinks nothing of lying in the rain and cold, thanks to his thick waterproof coat. While we shiver indoors, we know that if we attempt to close the door, he will push it wide open in his rush to see what he's missing. Leos are incredibly nosy dogs; they are always curious to know everything that is going on around them.

The Leonberger is a very agile breed, capable of turning on a dime. Unfortunately, the Leo's inability to come to a halt has caused many a bruised limb. It is often thought that this may be just a ploy by Leos to get their owners on the floor so they can give the dogs some special

the opportunity, swimming can be a most enjoyable experience. Dogs that have never swum before can take to it like a fish to water and, with training, can become as proficient at water rescue as another cousin, the Newfoundland.

THE WATER BOWL AND OTHER PECULIARITIES

The water bowl is a good indicator of the pup's level of development. At an early age, Leos have an affinity for water. As very young puppies, they love nothing more than to sleep with their heads in their water bowls. Breeders and owners often complain about not being able to keep their pups dry.

As well as the obvious visual

attention. (If someone is on the floor, the Leo cannot resist the temptation to lick furiously at the person's face.)

Leonbergers seem to have no idea of their size or exactly where their tails are, which is why Leo owners do not have coffee tables or put trinkets on lower shelves. Further, the Leonberger's height makes him think nothing of joining you and your guests for dinner. Resting his head on the table and looking from one person to the next with a fixed hypnotic gaze, he will make sure that at least one person will feel guilty enough to share his or her meal.

When a Leo feels he is not receiving the amount of attention he deserves, he will hold his head up high and look you straight in the eye. He will then shift his weight from one leg to the other as if standing on hot coals, and slowly make snake-like movements with his body. You will hear a sound that resembles a huffing noise crossed with a bark. When he has your full attention, he will walk backwards to let you know that his need is urgent. Once he has distracted you, and you walk towards him to see what the problem is, he will bounce a couple of times toward you, jubilant at having won your full attention.

Leonbergers are very dextrous with their feet, using them to pull things towards themselves rather than stretching and using up unnecessary energy. When a Leo wants to play with you or wants a cuddle, you will feel the full force of a paw hitting you until you give in and spend a few minutes attending to his wishes. Another favorite ploy is to prod you very

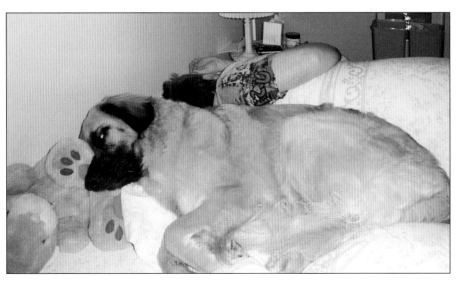

To the loyal and affectionate Leo, "close" is never "close enough" when it comes to being near those he loves.

hard in the back with his muzzle or to head-butt you between the legs, using you as a tunnel, a method that only has to work once for it to become an enjoyable habit for the Leo. For some reason known only to Leonbergers, a bitch has a tendency to use her toenails rather more than the genteel male. The nails are used to grab you in a way similar to that of a bird of prey's using its talons. You can imagine the pain inflicted when a Leo's nails are dragged down one's back during an overzealous greeting.

Leonbergers seem to enjoy being taught new things and are fast learners but, when competing with a Leonberger, whether it be in obedience, agility trials, flyball, etc., the Leo likes to calculate what is ahead of him and decide for

FAMOUS OWNERS
Many celebrities and royals have owned Leonbergers, including Robert Wagner, the Grand Duke Friedrich von Baden, Bismarck, Edward VII and Princess Stephanie of Monaco.

himself how to accomplish the task. Leos are generally very obedient but can set their own priorities, often with amusing results. One day a Leo named Barney was performing the sendaway exercise in a British obedience competition and was headed in a straight line toward the box when he suddenly veered off to the left. He continued in a direct line out of the ring over to a bush, had a sniff and relieved himself. He

Bramble and his young friends have some fun with the Leo's carting talents.

then returned to his original path, turned left straight into the box and lay down!

AMUSING ANECDOTES

As with all breeds, not everything comes naturally, and training is an essential part of looking after your Leonberger. They are fast learners when they want to be and are very capable of competing with the best when it comes to obedience. Yet they have a natural tendency to think about what they have been commanded to do and may deem it more important to investigate newly discovered scents than to respond immediately to their owners' commands.

Of course, Leos do learn quickly the things that they are not supposed to know: how to stand up on their hind legs and reach the food we thought was out of harm's way; how to open fridge doors; how to open baby gates that are supposed to keep them either in or out; which is the best armchair and where the best constant supply of water is (e.g., the toilet!). No doubt these are clever canines!

Most Leonberger owners have anecdotes illustrating the breed's wonderful sense of humor. None of these stories shows a sense of

A hungry Leo will help himself if he can get to the food...and not much is out of his reach.

A Leo family with happiness times three!

malice, only the Leo's ability to brighten anyone's day!

HARVEY

At his first obedience competition, during the retrieve exercise, Harvey proceeded to collect his very large, heavy dumbbell. On his return, he noticed a kindly lady (the judge) watching him, so he decided to share his gift with her. He sat beautifully in front of her and dropped the dumbbell on her foot. Failing to understand why the woman suddenly started hopping around on one leg, he picked up the dumbbell and returned to his owner.

ELSA

At her obedience class, Elsa was given the command to heel. She took the instruction literally and hung on to her owner's heel as they walked around the hall. During the scent training, she would seek out her owner's cloth, pick it up and, while promptly returning to her owner, swallow it! Once she was in the sit position, Elsa's mouth was pried open and her owner would reach into her throat and retrieve the somewhat soggy article. A spectacular retrieve!

FLYBALL FLOWER

A male Leo was competing at a flyball event. After clearing the jumps and just before correctly retrieving the ball from the box, he spotted a flower nearby. He picked the flower, returned over the jumps and presented a very embarrassed owner with his floral gift.

DOG WALKERS

Out on a walk with several people and their Leos, one Leo bitch spotted another group of walkers in the distance. She ran off and joined the other group, walking to heel with one of the people. When her owner called out for her, the dog ignored the call and looked to her new companions. On hearing the shouts, they noticed their new addition and stopped. Only by putting the lead back on the dog could the owner persuade her to leave her new friends. (Hint: Walk your Leo *on leash!)*

ABE

Abe loved the water, so when he came across the garden hose with water spouting from its nozzle, he took his prize indoors for safekeeping. His owner wasn't too happy when she paddled into the den!

AN ADDICTIVE BREED

Leonbergers make delightful pets and, like all breeds, they have their endearing peculiarities. They are an addictive breed, and very few Leonberger owners are content to have only one—a testimonial to the joys of owning the Leo!

A dog the size of the Leonberger can literally sweep someone off her feet!

LEONBERGER

In the 19th century, when the breed was first registered, records were kept so that breeders had guidelines to help them produce the correct type of dog. The Leonberger is not recognized by the American Kennel Club, so fanciers in the US look to the breed standard of the Leo's homeland, Germany. The German standard is that recognized by Europe's Fédération Cynologique Internationale (FCI), the "world kennel club."

Without the breed standard, we would have all types of dogs that breeders would claim to be Leonbergers. The standard describes to us what the Leonberger should look like—how long the body is, what coat length and color are desirable, how the head should be constructed, what is proper temperament, etc. If Herr Essig had not registered the breed and records had not been kept, we would have a very different dog today, perhaps not a Leonberger at all.

Every time a breeder decides to have a litter, the standard should be consulted as to whether or not the dog and bitch conform to type and temperament. There is

BETTER THAN THE AVERAGE DOG

Even though you may never show your dog, you should still read the breed standard. The breed standard tells you more than just physical specifications, such as how tall your dog should be; it also describes how he should act, how he should move and what unique qualities make him the breed that he is. You are not investing money in a pure-bred dog so that you can own a dog that "sort of looks like" the breed you're purchasing. You want a typical, handsome representative of the breed, one that all of your friends and family and people you meet out in public will recognize as the breed you've so carefully selected and researched. If the parents of your prospective puppy bear little or no resemblance in looks and/or personality to the dog described in the breed standard, you should keep searching!

never any guarantee that using what we consider to be correct-type dogs is going to produce good offspring, but as long as the standard is followed as closely as possible, we can hope that the results will be good.

Those people judging our dogs in the show ring must also know the standard. The judge's interpretation of the standard will decide the winner and thus determine future breed type. Dogs winning regularly will be favored as brood bitches or stud dogs, and so it is important that judges choose dogs that conform as closely as possible to correct breed type.

THE FCI BREED STANDARD FOR THE LEONBERGER
FCI Standard #145/20.09.2002/GB

TRANSLATION
Mrs. C. Seidler, revised by Mrs. E. Peper.

ORIGIN
Germany.

DATE OF PUBLICATION OF THE ORIGINAL VALID STANDARD
04.01.1996.

UTILIZATION
Watch, Companion and Family Dog.

Best in Show winners at a Leonberger Club show, along with their handlers and the judges.

Here is Kiseirdi Nora, an International Champion and German club winner, as well as dam and granddam to top-winning Leos.

FCI CLASSIFICATION
Group 2, Pinscher and Schnauzer, Molossoid breeds, Swiss Mountain and Cattle Dogs and other breeds. Section 2.2, Molossoid breeds, Mountain type. Without working trial.

BRIEF HISTORICAL SUMMARY
At the end of the thirties, beginning of the forties of the 19th century, Heinrich Essig, town Councilor in Leonberg near Stuttgart, crossed a black and white Newfoundland bitch with a so-called "Barry" male from the monastery hospice Grand St. Bernhard. Later a Pyrenean Mountain Dog was added. This resulted in very large dogs with predominantly long, white coats. Essig's aim was for a lion-like dog. The lion is the heraldic animal of the city of Leonberg. The first dogs really called "Leonbergers" were born in 1846. They combined the excellent qualities of the breeds from which they stemmed. Only a short time later, many of these dogs were sold as status symbols from Leonberg all over the world. At the end of the 19th century, the Leonberger was kept in Baden-Württemberg as the preferred farm dog. His watch and draft abilities were much praised. In both World Wars and the needy post-war times, the numbers of breeding stock reduced dramatically. Today the Leonberger is an excellent family dog which fulfills all the demands of modern life.

GENERAL APPEARANCE
According to his original purpose, the Leonberger is a large, strong, muscular yet elegant dog. He is distinguished by his balanced build and confident calmness, yet with quite a lively temperament. Males, in particular, are powerful and strong.

IMPORTANT PROPORTIONS
Height at the withers to length of body: 9 to 10. The depth of chest is nearly 50% of the height at withers.

BEHAVIOR/TEMPERAMENT
As a family dog, the Leonberger is an agreeable partner for present-day dwelling and living conditions, who can be taken anywhere without difficulty and is distinguished by his marked friendliness towards children. He is neither shy nor aggressive. As a companion, he is agreeable, obedient and fearless in all situations of life. The following are particular requirements of steady temperament:
• Self assurance and superior composure.
• Medium temperament (including playfulness).
• Willing to be submissive.
• Good capacity for learning and remembering.
• Insensitive to noise.

HEAD
On the whole deeper than broad and elongated rather than stocky. Proportion of length of muzzle to length of skull: about 1 to 1. Skin close fitting all over, no wrinkles.
Cranial Region: Skull: In profile and seen from the front, slightly arched. In balance with body and limbs, it is strong but not heavy. The skull at its back part is not substantially broader than near the eyes. Stop: Clearly recognizable but moderately defined.
Facial Region: Nose: Black. Muzzle: Rather long, never running to a point; nasal bridge of even breadth, never dipped, rather slightly arched (roman nose). Lips: Close fitting, black, corners of lips closed. Jaws/Teeth: Strong jaws with a perfect, regular and complete scissor bite, the upper teeth closely overlapping the lower teeth without any gap, and teeth set square to the jaw with 42 sound teeth according to the dentition formula (missing M3 tolerated). Pincer bite is accepted; no constriction at the canines in the lower jaw. Cheeks: Only slightly developed. Eyes: Light brown to as dark brown as possible, medium size, oval, neither deep set, nor protruding, neither too close together nor too wide apart. Eyelids close fitting, not showing any conjunctiva. The white of the eye (the visible part of the sclera) not reddened. Ears: Set on high and not far back, pendant, of medium size, hanging close to the head, fleshy.

NECK
Running in a slight curve without break to the withers. Somewhat long rather than stocky, without throatiness or dewlap.

BODY
Withers: Pronounced, especially in males. Back: Firm, straight, broad.

Shermayne Daangertin at Tariqoba, bred by the author and proudly owned by Fran Williams.

Mattheleen First in Line, taking first in his class.

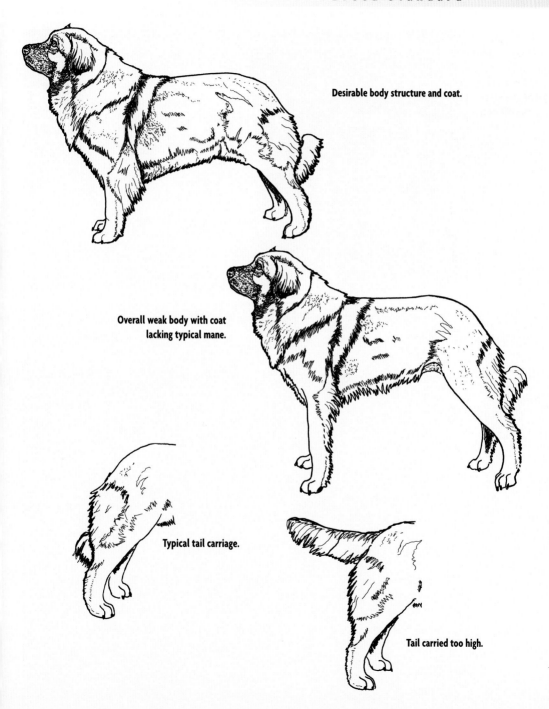

Desirable body structure and coat.

Overall weak body with coat lacking typical mane.

Typical tail carriage.

Tail carried too high.

Loins: Broad, strong, well muscled. Croup: Broad, relatively long, gently rounded, flowing to merge with tail set on; never overbuilt. Chest: Broad, deep, reaching at least to the level of the elbows. Not too barrel shaped, more oval. Underline and belly: Only slightly tucked up.

TAIL

Very well furnished; while standing, it hangs down straight; also in movement it is only slightly curved and if at all possible should not be carried above the prolongation of the topline.

LIMBS

Very strong, especially in males.

Forequarters: Forelegs straight, parallel and not too close. Shoulders/Upper arm: Long, sloping, forming a not too blunt angle, well muscled. Elbows: Close

to the body. Pastern: Strong, firm; seen from the front, straight; almost vertical, seen from the side. Forefeet: Straight (turning neither in nor out), rounded, tight, toes well arched; black pads.

Hindquarters: Seen from the rear, position of the hind legs not too close, parallel. Hocks and feet: Turned neither in nor out. Pelvis: Slanting. Upper thigh: Rather long, slanting, strongly muscled. Upper and lower thigh form a distinct angle. Hocks: Strong, distinct angle between lower thigh and rear pastern. Hind feet: Standing straight, only slightly longish. Toes arched, pads black.

GAIT/MOVEMENT

Ground-covering even movement in all gaits. Extending well in front with good drive from the hindquarters. Seen from front and behind the limbs move in a straight line when walking or trotting.

COAT

Hair: Medium soft to coarse, profusely long, close fitting, never parted, with the shape of the whole body visible despite the thick undercoat. Straight, slight wave still permitted; forming a mane on neck and chest, especially in males; distinct feathering on front legs and ample breeches on hind legs.

Color: Lion yellow, red, reddish brown, also sandy (pale

yellow, cream colored) and all combinations in between, always with a black mask. Black hair tips are permitted; however, black must not determine the dog's basic color. Lightening up of the basic color on the underside of the tail, the mane, the feathering on the front legs and the breeches on the hind legs must not be so pronounced as to interfere with the harmony of the main color. A small white patch or stripe on the chest and white hairs on the toes are tolerated.

SIZE
Height at the withers: Dogs: 72 to 80 cm (recommended average 76 cm). Bitches: 65 to 75 cm (recommended average 70 cm).

FAULTS
Any departure from the foregoing points should be considered a fault and the seriousness with which the fault should be regarded should be in exact proportion to its degree.

DISQUALIFYING FAULTS
- Shy or aggressive dogs.
- Severe anatomical faults (i.e., pronounced cow hocks, pronounced roach back, bad swayback; front feet turning out extremely. Totally insufficient angulation of shoulder, elbow, stifle or hock joints.
- Brown nose leather.
- Very strong lack of pigment in lips.

- Absence of teeth (with the exception of M3). Over- or undershot or other faults in mouth.
- Eyes without any brown.
- Entropion, ectropion.
- Distinct ring tail or too highly curled up tail.
- Brown pads.
- Cords or strong curls.
- Faulty colors (brown with brown nose and brown pads; black and tan; black; silver; wild-coat color).
- Complete lack of mask.
- Too much white (reaching from toes onto pasterns), white on chest larger than palm of hand, white in other places.

N.B.: Male animals should have two apparently normal testicles fully descended into the scrotum.

Swedish Ch. Dragongardens Rival won a Club Show Certificate and was awarded Best Male out of a field of 110 dogs.

LEONBERGER

HOW TO SELECT A LEO PUPPY

As with any breed, it is important to research the particular breed in which you are interested to make certain that it is suited to your lifestyle. Try meeting some adult dogs in their home environment. Consider the size of the Leonberger and determine if your home is large enough to accommodate a fully-grown Leo. A Leo can take up a lot of space when lying on the floor; plus, you will need room for his crate and bedding.

Can you afford to feed and insure this large dog against any unforeseen illnesses or accidents? Due to the breed's great size, veterinary expenses are far greater than those of a small- or medium-sized dog. Do you go out to work? You should not even consider purchasing a puppy if you (or

> ### SIGNS OF A HEALTHY PUPPY
> Healthy puppies are robust little fellows who are alert and active, sporting shiny coats and supple skin. They should not appear lethargic, bloated or pot-bellied, nor should they have flaky skin or runny or crusted eyes or noses. Their stools should be firm and well formed, with no evidence of blood or mucus.

someone in the family) are not going to be at home to look after him, as the sensitive and intelligent Leonberger craves human companionship and mental stimulation. Leaving a dog alone for hours on end would be unbearable for the Leo.

Young puppies can do a lot of damage indoors and in the yard, especially when teething. Some have been known to consume entire three-piece suits, moldings and doors. Others will chew walls through to the brickwork. Leos are exceedingly good at digging and, left to their own devices, will excavate craters in your beautifully tended lawn, devouring your

A curious Leo puppy is always on the move.

shrubs and flowers. They will tread mud into your home and shake it all over your furniture. In wet weather, will you be happy to have a wet soggy dog to be continuously cleaning up after? Further, Leonbergers love water, be it in the form of rain, dirty puddles, baths or drinking vessels. You can count on always having wet floors and an abundance of hair that settles everywhere.

So, if you still want a Leonberger after those considerations, the next thing to do would be to find some reputable breeders. You can do this by contacting the Leonberger Club of America. They can refer you to breeders and put you in touch with other owners so that you may get advice and see Leos in their home environments.

There are definite advantages to buying a puppy from an LCA member breeder. Knowing that LCA breeders abide by the club's strict ethics and breeding regula-

tions, thereby ensuring the health and temperament of their dogs to the best of their ability, must be a comforting thought to any potential puppy owner. You still must be comfortable with your breeder; it is helpful if you get along with the breeder personally. You don't have to commit to the first breeder you meet—take your time, do some research, talk to people in the breed and visit some different breeders and litters. A dog show can be a good opportunity to see Leonbergers in action and to talk to breeders, handlers and owners.

The Leo puppy can fit nicely in a corner of the sofa...but it won't be long until there's no room for anyone else!

FINDING A QUALIFIED BREEDER

Before you begin your puppy search, ask for references from the breed club, your vet and perhaps other breeders to refer you to someone they believe is reputable. Responsible breeders usually raise only one or two breeds of dog. Avoid any breeder who has several different breeds or has several litters at the same time. Dedicated breeders are usually involved with their breed club and possibly other dog clubs. Many participate in some sport or activity related to their breed. Just as you want to be assured of the breeder's qualifications, a good breeder wants to be assured that you will make a worthy owner. Expect the breeder to interview you, asking questions about your goals for the pup, your experience with dogs and what kind of home you will provide.

A quartet of six-week-old Stormchaser pups; two females (top of photo) and two males. Imagine how difficult it would be to choose!

Considering that there are certain hereditary concerns in the Leonberger breed, you are advised to be cautious of these concerns at the time of purchase. Before you agree to buy a puppy or leave a deposit, it is of great importance

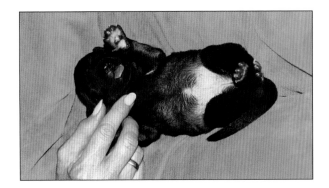

GETTING ACQUAINTED

When visiting a litter, ask the breeder for suggestions on how best to interact with the puppies. If possible, get right into the middle of the pack and sit down with them. Observe which pups climb into your lap and which ones shy away. Toss a toy for them to chase and bring back to you. It's easy to fall in love with the puppy who picks you, but keep your future objectives in mind before you make your final decision.

that you ask to see the documents relating to the hip grades, elbow grades and eye tests of the sire and dam of that puppy. If the breeder cannot produce these documents, do not buy the puppy! The Orthopedic Foundation for Animals (OFA) and the Canine Eye Registration Foundation (CERF) provide testing and clearances for dogs with healthy hips, elbows and eyes. Further, the breeder should be willing to discuss these and other potential health problems in the breed.

You also need to see the dam and possibly the sire of the litter that you are viewing. Are they good examples of the breed and, of utmost importance, do they have excellent temperaments? Some breeders even participate in formal temperament testing. Assuming that everything is as it should be with the parents—good hip and elbow grades, eyes tested clear and sound temperaments— you then need to know that the

Can you believe that a Leonberger starts out this small?

Quality pups come from quality breeding. Here is busy mom Storm with some of her six-week-old pups...there were twelve in this litter!

breeder is going to supply you with the necessary paperwork at the time of purchasing the puppy. These documents include the puppy's pedigree and health records, a diet sheet, the breeder's sales contract and after-sale support. You need to know that you can contact the breeder for help and advice when problems arise.

The next step is to choose your puppy. Look for clean bright eyes and a moist cold nose. Watch the litter and notice if any pups are particularly quiet, as they may be ill. Are any of the puppies lame when moving about? Ask if any have umbilical hernias, as sometimes Leos do, and if they need veterinary attention. Avoid sickly-looking puppies, those with weepy eyes or any discharge around the eyes and nostrils, and puppies that seem nervous. Stay away from any litter that doesn't

look clean and healthy. If in doubt about anything, consult your vet and, if the vet cannot give you the answer to the problem, ask the breed club for advice.

When studying the conformation of the puppies, choose an attractive head with broad muzzle, a straight topline, straight front legs, good angulation of the hind legs, a long tail and good free movement. Ask someone who knows the breed to view the litter with you if you are unsure of what to look for. Even though you may spend hours choosing a puppy and following all the right advice, there is never any guarantee that your puppy will turn out to be a perfect specimen. If you are choosing a Leo pup as a pet and do not intend to show him, you do not have to pick a conformationally "perfect" specimen.

PUPPY PARASITES

Parasites are nasty little critters that live in or on your dog or puppy. Most puppies are born with ascarid roundworms, which are acquired from dormant ascarids residing in the dam. Other parasites can be acquired through contact with infected fecal matter. Take a stool sample to your vet for testing. He will prescribe a safe wormer to treat any parasites found in your puppy's stool. Always have a fecal test performed at your puppy's annual veterinary exam.

However, whether pet puppy or show prospect, overall soundness, health and temperament are of utmost importance.

A COMMITTED NEW OWNER

By now you should understand what makes the Leonberger a most unique and special dog, one that may fit nicely into your family and lifestyle. If you have researched breeders, you should be able to recognize a knowledge-able and responsible Leonberger breeder who cares not only about his pups but also about what kind of owner you will be. If you have completed the final step in your new journey, you have found a litter, or possibly two, of quality Leonberger pups.

A visit with the puppies and their breeder should be an education in itself. Breed research, breeder selection and puppy visitation are very important aspects of finding the puppy of your dreams. Beyond that, these things also lay the foundation for a successful future with your pup. Puppy personalities within each litter vary, from the shy and easygoing puppy to the one who is dominant and assertive, with most pups falling somewhere in between. By spending time with the puppies you will be able to recognize certain behaviors and what these behaviors indicate about each pup's temperament. Which type of pup will complement your family dynamics is best determined by observing the puppies in action within their "pack." Your breeder's expertise and recommendations are also valuable. Although you may fall in love with a bold and brassy

Eight-week-old littermates, Shermayne Berealls Galaxy at Stormchaser (bitch) and Shermayne Braga Ferengi at Stormchaser (dog).

male, the breeder may suggest that another pup would be best for you. The breeder's experience in rearing Leonberger pups and matching their temperaments with appropriate humans offers the best assurance that your pup will meet your needs and expectations. The type of puppy that you select is just as important as your decision that the Leonberger is the breed for you.

The decision to live with a Leonberger is a serious commitment and not one to be taken lightly. This puppy is a living sentient being that will be dependent on you for basic survival for his entire life. Beyond the basics of survival—food, water, shelter and protection—he needs much, much more. The new pup needs love, nurturing and a proper canine education to mold him into a responsible, well-behaved canine citizen. Your Leonberger's health and good manners will need consistent monitoring and regular "tune-ups," so your job as a responsible dog owner will be ongoing throughout every stage of his life. If you are not prepared to accept these responsibilities and commit to them for the next decade, likely longer, then you are not prepared to own a dog of any breed.

Although the responsibilities of owning a dog may at times tax your patience, the joy of living with your Leonberger far outweighs the workload, and a well-mannered adult dog is worth your time and effort. Before your very eyes, your new charge will be your most loyal friend and companion, devoted to you unconditionally.

THE FAMILY TREE

Your puppy's pedigree is his family tree. Just as a child may resemble his parents and grandparents, so too will a puppy reflect the qualities, good and bad, of his ancestors, especially those in the first two generations. Therefore it's important to know as much as possible about a puppy's immediate relatives. Reputable and experienced breeders should be able to explain the pedigree and why they chose to breed from the particular dogs they used.

YOUR LEONBERGER SHOPPING LIST

Just as expectant parents prepare a nursery for their baby, so should you ready your home for the arrival of your Leonberger pup. If you have the necessary puppy supplies purchased and in place before he comes home, it will ease the puppy's transition from the warmth and familiarity of his mom and littermates to the brand-new environment of his new home and human family. You will be too busy to stock up and prepare your house after your pup comes home, that's for sure! Imagine how a pup must feel upon being transported to a strange new place. It's up to you to comfort him and to let your little pup know that he is going to be happy with you.

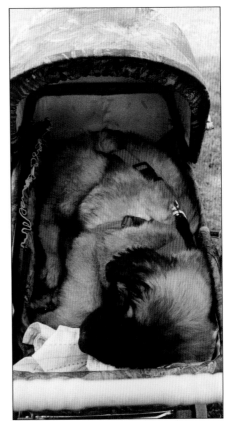

Eight-week-old Fitzwilliam is truly babied by his owner, who took him out for early socialization from the safety of a carriage.

FOOD AND WATER BOWLS

Your puppy will need separate bowls for his food and water. Stainless steel pans are generally preferred over plastic bowls since they sterilize better and pups are less inclined to chew on the

When it comes to the Leo's bowls, the larger, heavier and sturdier, the better.

Pups should look inquisitive and alert, as demonstrated by young Stormchaser Shooting Star.

metal. Heavy-duty ceramic bowls are also popular. Your Leo will be fixated on his water bowl, so purchase the largest, sturdiest one you can find. Your puppy will grow into the large bowls before you know it.

THE DOG CRATE

If you think that crates are tools of punishment and confinement for when a dog has misbehaved, think again. Many breeders and almost all trainers recommend a crate as the preferred house-training aid as well as for all-around puppy training and safety. Because dogs are natural den creatures that prefer cave-like environments, the benefits of crate use are many. The crate provides the puppy with his very own "safe house," a cozy place to sleep, take a break or seek comfort

with a favorite toy; a travel aid to house your dog when on the road, at motels or at the vet's office; a training aid to help teach your puppy proper toileting habits; a place of solitude when non-dog people happen to drop by and don't want a lively puppy—or even a well-behaved adult dog—saying hello or begging for attention.

Crates come in several types, although the wire crate and the fiberglass airline-type crate are the most common. Do not purchase an enclosed fiberglass crate, since your Leo will hate it! Remember, Leos are nosy and proud of it. They must know what is going on around them, and a wire crate gives them a view of their whole surroundings, plus provides better ventalation than an enclosed crate. Many of the wire crates easily fold down for easy transport.

CONFINEMENT

It is wise to keep your puppy confined to a small "puppy-proofed" area of the house for his first few weeks at home. Gate or block off a space near the door he will use for outdoor potty trips. Expandable baby gates are useful to create puppy's designated area. If he is allowed to roam through the entire house or even only several rooms, it will be more difficult to house-train him.

Examples of mesh (left), wire (right) and fiberglass (top) crates. A large wire crate is the best choice for a Leo.

Some of the newer crates are made of heavy plastic mesh; they are very lightweight and fold up into slim-line suitcases. However, a mesh crate might not be suitable for a pup with manic chewing habits and may not be sturdy enough for the strong Leo.

As far as purchasing a crate for the Leonberger, you will have to purchase the largest wire crate you can order. Since the adult Leo can stand up to 31.5 inches at the shoulder, you will need to give him enough space to keep him comfortable.

BEDDING AND CRATE PADS
Your puppy will enjoy some type of soft bedding in his "room" (the crate), something he can snuggle into to feel cozy and secure. Old towels or blankets are good choices for a young pup, since he may (and probably will) have a toileting accident or two in the crate or decide to chew on the bedding material. Once he is fully trained and out of the early chewing stage, you can replace the puppy bedding with a permanent crate pad if you prefer. Crate pads and other dog beds run the gamut from inexpensive to

Whispering sweet nothings—it must be puppy love!

TOYS 'R SAFE

The vast array of tantalizing puppy toys is staggering. Stroll through any pet shop or pet-supply outlet and you will see that the choices can be overwhelming. However, not all dog toys are safe or sensible. Most very young puppies enjoy soft woolly toys that they can snuggle with and carry around. (You know they have outgrown them when they shred them up!) Avoid toys that have buttons, tabs or other enhancements that can be chewed off and swallowed. Soft toys that squeak are fun, but make sure your puppy does not disembowel the toy and remove (and swallow) the squeaker. Toys that rattle or make noise can excite a puppy, but they present the same danger as the squeaky kind and so require supervision. Hard rubber toys that bounce can also entertain a pup, but make sure that the toy is too big for your pup to swallow.

high-end doggie-designer styles, but don't splurge on the good stuff until you are sure that your puppy is reliable and won't tear it up or make a mess on it.

PUPPY TOYS

Just as infants and older children require objects to stimulate their minds and bodies, puppies need toys to entertain their curious brains, wiggly paws and achy teeth. A fun array of safe doggie toys will help satisfy your puppy's chewing instincts and hopefully distract him from gnawing on the leg of your antique chair or your new leather sofa. Most puppy toys are cute and look as if they would be a lot of fun, but not all are necessarily safe or good for your puppy, so use caution when you go puppy-toy shopping.

Leo puppies are aggressive chewers. They love to chew! The best "chewcifiers" are nylon and hard rubber bones; many are safe to gnaw on and come in sizes appropriate for all age groups and breeds. Be especially careful of natural bones, which can splinter or develop dangerous sharp edges; pups can easily swallow or choke on those bone splinters. Veterinarians often tell of surgical nightmares involving bits of splintered bone, because in addition to the danger of choking, the sharp pieces can damage the intestinal tract.

Similarly, rawhide chews, while a favorite of most dogs and puppies, can be equally dangerous. Pieces of rawhide are easily swallowed after they get soft and gummy from chewing, and dogs have been known to choke on large pieces of ingested rawhide. Rawhide chews should be offered only when you can supervise the puppy.

Soft woolly toys are special puppy favorites. They come in a wide variety of cute shapes and sizes; some look like little stuffed animals. Puppies love to shake them up and toss them about, or simply carry them around. Be careful of fuzzy toys that have button eyes or noses that your

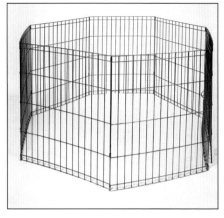

An exercise pen, also known as an "ex-pen," is a helpful tool in keeping a pup confined to a puppy-proof area. An adult Leo, however, is not contained as easily in a pen with short sides.

pup could chew off and swallow, and make sure that he does not disembowel a squeaky toy to remove the squeaker! Braided rope toys are similar in that they are fun to chew and toss around, but they shred easily and the strings are easy to swallow. The strings are not digestible and, if the puppy doesn't pass them in his stool, he could end up at the vet's office. As with rawhides, your puppy should be closely monitored with rope toys.

If you believe that your pup has ingested a piece of one of his toys, check his stools for the next couple of days to see if he passes the item when he defecates. At the same time, also watch for signs of intestinal distress. A call to your veterinarian might be in order to get his advice and be on the safe side.

An all-time favorite toy for puppies (young and old!) is the empty gallon milk jug. Hard

TEETHING TIME

All puppies chew. It's normal canine behavior. Chewing just plain feels good to a puppy, especially during the three- to five-month teething period when the adult teeth are breaking through the gums. Rather than attempting to eliminate such a strong natural chewing instinct, you will be more successful if you redirect it and teach your puppy what he may or may not chew. Correct inappropriate chewing with a sharp "No!" and offer him a chew toy, praising him when he takes it. Don't become discouraged. Your Leo's chewing should decrease after the adult teeth have come in.

plastic juice containers—46 ounces or more—are also excellent. Such containers make lots of noise when they are batted about, and puppies go crazy with delight as they play with them. However, these won't last more than a few minutes with a Leo, so be sure to remove and replace them as soon as they get chewed up.

A word of caution about homemade toys: be careful with your choices of non-traditional play objects. Never use old shoes or socks, since a puppy cannot distinguish between the old ones on which he's allowed to chew and the new ones in your closet that are strictly off limits. That principle applies to anything that resembles something that you don't want your puppy to chew

up. Remember, the Leo will chew on anything from shoes to tables to walls.

COLLARS

A lightweight nylon collar is the best choice for a very young pup. Quick-clip collars are easy to put on and remove, and they can be adjusted as the puppy grows. Introduce him to his collar as soon as he comes home to get him accustomed to wearing it. He'll get used to it quickly and won't mind a bit. Make sure that it is snug enough that it won't slip off, yet loose enough to be comfortable for the pup. You should be able to slip two fingers between the collar and his neck. Check the collar often, as puppies grow in spurts, and his collar can become too tight almost overnight. Consider also that the Leo's collar

Collaring Our Canines

The standard flat collar with a buckle or a snap, in leather, nylon or cotton, is widely regarded as the everyday all-purpose collar. If the collar fits correctly, you should be able to fit two fingers between the collar and the dog's neck.

Leather Buckle Collars

Limited-Slip Collar

The martingale, Greyhound or limited-slip collar is preferred by many dog owners and trainers. It is fixed with an extra loop that tightens when pressure is applied to the leash. The martingale collar gets tighter but does not "choke" the dog. The limited-slip collar should only be used for walking and training, not for free play or interaction with another dog. These types of collar should never be left on the dog, as the extra loop can lead to accidents.

Choke collars, usually made of stainless steel, are made for training purposes but are not recommended for small dogs or heavily coated breeds like the Leo. The chains can injure small dogs or damage long/abundant coats. Thin nylon choke leads are commonly used on show dogs while in the ring, though they are not practical for everyday use.

Snap Bolt Choke Collar

The harness, with two or three straps that attach over the dog's shoulders and around his torso, is a humane and safe alternative to the conventional collar. By and large, a well-made harness is virtually escape-proof. Harnesses are available in nylon and mesh and can be outfitted on most dogs, with chest girths ranging from 10 to 30 inches.

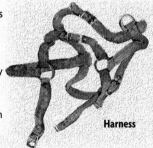

Harness

Nylon Collar

Quick-Click Closure

Snake Chain

Chrome Steel

Fur-Saver

Choke Chain Collars

A head collar, composed of a nylon strap that goes around the dog's muzzle and a second strap that wraps around his neck, offers the owner better control over his dog. This device is recommended for problem-solving with dogs (including jumping up, pulling and aggressive behaviors), but must be used with care.

A training halter, including a flat collar and two straps, made of nylon and webbing, is designed for walking. There are several on the market; some are more difficult to put on the dog than others. The halter harness, with two small slip rings at each end, is recommended for ease of use.

must fit comfortably over his thick coat. Choke collars are not recommended for the Leo at any age. Training collars should not be used on puppies, young dogs/adults that pull on the leash can use a leather "half-check" collar, which is gentler than a choke and won't damage the coat.

LEASHES

A 6-foot nylon lead is an excellent choice for a young puppy. It is lightweight and not as tempting to chew as a leather lead. You can switch to a 6-foot leather lead after your pup has grown and is used to walking politely on a lead. For initial puppy walks and house-training purposes, you should invest in a shorter lead so that you have more control over the puppy. At first, you don't want him wandering too far away from you, and when taking him out for toileting you will want to keep him in the specific area chosen for his potty spot.

HOME SAFETY FOR YOUR PUPPY

The importance of puppy-proofing cannot be overstated. In addition to making your house comfortable for your Leonberger's arrival, you also must make sure that your house is safe for your puppy before you bring him home. There are countless hazards in the owner's personal living environment that a pup can sniff,

TOXIC PLANTS

Plants are natural puppy magnets, but many can be harmful, even fatal, if ingested by a puppy or adult dog. Scout your yard and home interior and remove any plants, bushes or flowers that could be even mildly dangerous. It could save your puppy's life. You can obtain a complete list of toxic plants from your veterinarian, at the public library or by looking online.

chew, swallow or destroy. Many are obvious; others are not. Do a thorough advance house check to remove or rearrange those things that could hurt your puppy, keeping any potentially dangerous items out of areas to which he will have access. Most Leonberger owners remove small tables from their homes, as, believe it or not, Leos tend to eat them! They can also easily grab items or knock things off of lower tables and shelves, and more becomes reachable as they grow taller.

Electrical cords are especially dangerous, since puppies view them as irresistible chew toys. Unplug and remove all exposed cords or fasten them beneath a baseboard where the puppy cannot reach them. Veterinarians and firefighters can tell you horror stories about electrical burns and house fires that resulted from puppy-chewed electrical cords.

Leash Life

Dogs love leashes! Believe it or not, most dogs dance for joy every time their owners pick up their leashes. The leash means that the dog is going for a walk—and there are few things more exciting than that! Here are some of the kinds of leashes that are commercially available.

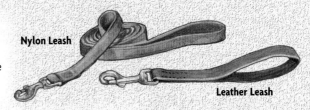

Nylon Leash

Leather Leash

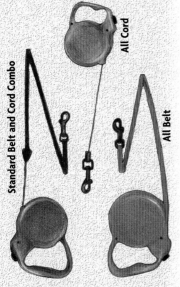

Standard Belt and Cord Combo

All Cord

All Belt

Retractable Leashes

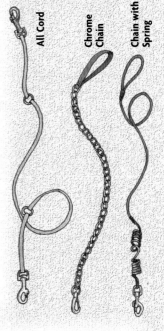

All Cord

Chrome Chain

Chain with Spring

Traditional Leash: Made of cotton, nylon or leather, these leashes are usually about 6 feet in length. A quality-made leather leash is softer on the hands than a nylon one. Durable woven cotton is a popular option. Lengths can vary up to about 48 feet, designed for different uses.

Chain Leash: Usually a metal chain leash with a plastic handle. This is not the best choice for most breeds, as it is heavier than other leashes and difficult to manage.

Retractable Leash: A long nylon cord is housed in a plastic device for extending and retracting. This type of leash is ideal for taking trained dogs for long walks in open areas, although it is not always suitable for large, powerful breeds. Different lengths and sizes are available, so check that you purchase one appropriate for your dog's weight.

Elastic Leash: A nylon leash with an elastic extension. This is useful for well-trained dogs, especially in conjunction with a head halter.

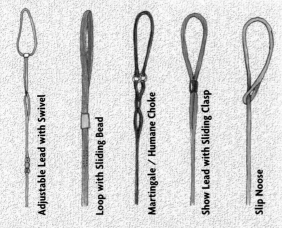

Adjustable Lead with Swivel

Loop with Sliding Bead

Martingale / Humane Choke

Show Lead with Sliding Clasp

Slip Noose

A Variety of Collar-and-Leash-in-One Products

Avoid leashes that are completely elastic, as they afford minimal control to the handler.

Adjustable Leash: This has two snaps, one on each end, and several metal rings. It is handy if you need to tether your dog temporarily, but is never to be used with a choke collar.

Tab Leash: A short leash (4 to 6 inches long) that attaches to your dog's collar. This device serves like a handle, in case you have to grab your dog while he's exercising off lead. It's ideal for "half-trained" dogs or dogs that listen only half of the time.

Slip Leash: Essentially a leash with a collar built in, similar to what a dog-show handler uses to show a dog. This British-style collar has a ring on the end so that you can form a slip collar. Useful if you have to catch your own runaway dog or a stray.

BE CONSISTENT

Consistency is a key element, in fact is absolutely necessary, to a puppy's learning environment. A behavior (such as chewing, jumping up or climbing onto the furniture) cannot be forbidden one day and then allowed the next. That will only confuse the pup, and he will not understand what he is supposed to do. Just one or two episodes of allowing an undesirable behavior to "slide" will imprint that behavior on a puppy's brain and make that behavior more difficult to erase or change.

A puppy resting by the hearth makes a charming photo, but an open fireplace can be a hazard. Identify potential puppy dangers before bringing the pup home.

Consider this a most serious precaution for your puppy and the rest of your family.

Scout your home for tiny objects that might be seen at a pup's eye level. Keep medication bottles and cleaning supplies well out of reach, and do the same with waste baskets and other trash containers. It goes without saying

that you should not use rodent poison or other toxic chemicals in any puppy area and that you must keep such containers safely locked up. You will be amazed at how many places a curious puppy can discover!

Once your house has cleared inspection, check your yard. A sturdy fence, well embedded into the ground, will give your dog a safe place to play and potty. Although Leonbergers are not known to be climbers or fence jumpers, they are still athletic dogs, so a 5- to 6-foot-high fence should be adequate to contain an agile youngster or adult. Check the fence periodically for necessary repairs. If there is a weak link or space to squeeze through or dig under, you can be sure a determined Leonberger will discover it.

The garage and shed can be hazardous places for a pup, as things like fertilizers, chemicals and tools are usually kept there. It's best to keep these areas off limits to the pup. Antifreeze is especially dangerous to dogs, as they find the taste appealing and it takes only a few licks from the driveway to kill a dog, puppy or adult, small breed or large.

VISITING THE VETERINARIAN

A good veterinarian is your Leonberger puppy's best health-insurance policy. If you do not already have a vet, ask friends and

A Dog-Safe Home

The dog-safety police are taking you and your new puppy on a house tour. Let's go room by room and see how safe your own home is for your new pup. The following items are doggie dangers, so either they must be removed or the dog should be monitored or not allowed access to these areas.

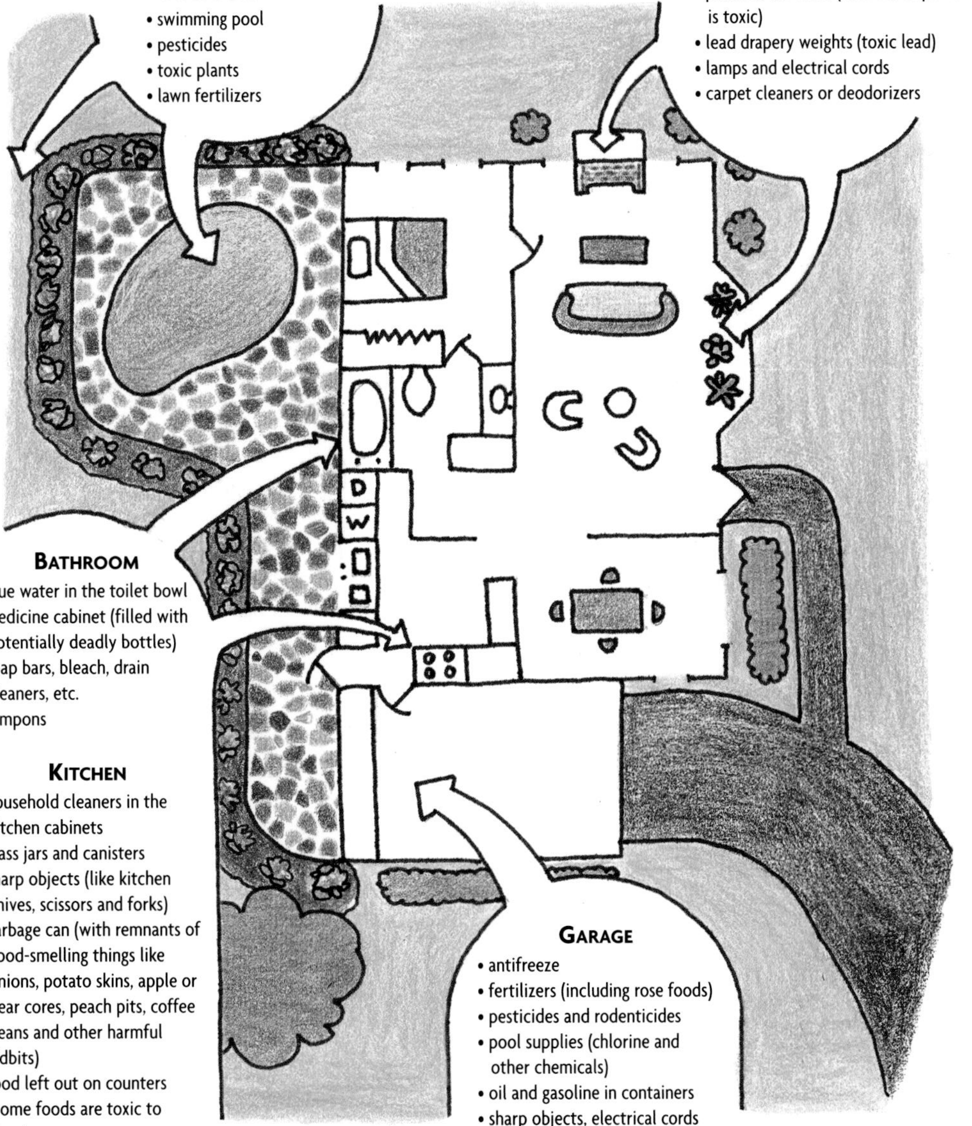

Living Room

- house plants (some varieties are poisonous)
- fireplace or wood-burning stove
- paint on the walls (lead-based paint is toxic)
- lead drapery weights (toxic lead)
- lamps and electrical cords
- carpet cleaners or deodorizers

Outdoors

- swimming pool
- pesticides
- toxic plants
- lawn fertilizers

Bathroom

- blue water in the toilet bowl
- medicine cabinet (filled with potentially deadly bottles)
- soap bars, bleach, drain cleaners, etc.
- tampons

Kitchen

- household cleaners in the kitchen cabinets
- glass jars and canisters
- sharp objects (like kitchen knives, scissors and forks)
- garbage can (with remnants of good-smelling things like onions, potato skins, apple or pear cores, peach pits, coffee beans and other harmful tidbits)
- food left out on counters (some foods are toxic to dogs)

Garage

- antifreeze
- fertilizers (including rose foods)
- pesticides and rodenticides
- pool supplies (chlorine and other chemicals)
- oil and gasoline in containers
- sharp objects, electrical cords and power tools

experienced dog people in your area for recommendations so that you can select a vet before you bring your Leonberger puppy home. Perhaps the breeder can recommend someone in the area who specializes in giant breeds. It is important that your chosen vet not be intimidated by large breeds and that he know about caring for giant dogs. Also arrange for your puppy's first veterinary examination beforehand, since many vets will not have appointments available right away and your puppy should visit the vet within a day or so of coming home.

It's important to make sure your puppy's first visit to the vet is a pleasant and positive one. The vet should take great care to befriend the pup and handle him

ASK THE VET

Help your vet help you to become a well-informed dog owner. Don't be shy about becoming involved in your puppy's veterinary care by asking questions and gaining as much knowledge as you can. For starters, ask what shots your puppy is getting and what diseases they prevent, and discuss with your vet the safest way to vaccinate. Find out what is involved in your dog's annual wellness visits. If you plan to spay or neuter, discuss the best age at which to have this done. Start out on the right "paw" with your puppy's vet and develop good communication with him, as he will care for your dog's health throughout the dog's entire life.

Leos love the outdoors! Your puppy will look forward to exploring his new back yard.

gently to make their first meeting a positive experience. The vet will give the pup a thorough physical examination and set up a schedule for vaccinations and other necessary wellness visits. Be sure to show your vet any health and inoculation records, which you should have received from your breeder. Your vet is a great source of canine health information, so be sure to ask questions and take notes. Creating a health journal for your puppy will make a handy reference for his wellness and any future health problems that may arise.

"What is this? Let's taste and find out!" A puppy will chew on almost anything, and he doesn't know what is harmful and what isn't...it's your job to keep him safe.

FIRST CAR RIDE

The ride to your home from the breeder will no doubt be your puppy's first automobile experience, and you should make every effort to keep him comfortable and secure. Bring a large towel or small blanket for the puppy to lie on during the trip and an extra towel in case the pup gets carsick or has a potty accident. It's best to have another person with you to hold the puppy in his lap. Most puppies will fall fast asleep from the rolling motion of the car. If the ride is lengthy, you may have to stop so that the puppy can relieve himself, so be sure to bring a leash and collar for those stops. Avoid rest areas for potty trips, since those are frequented by many dogs, who may carry parasites or disease. It's better to stop at grassy areas near gas stations or shopping centers to prevent unhealthy exposure for your pup.

MEETING THE FAMILY

Your Leonberger's homecoming is an exciting time for all members of the family, and it's only natural that everyone will be eager to meet him, pet him and play with him. However, for the puppy's sake, it's best to make these initial family meetings as uneventful as possible so that the pup is not overwhelmed with too much too soon. Remember, he has just left his dam and his littermates and is away from the breeder's home for the first time. Despite his fuzzy wagging tail, he is still apprehensive and wondering where he is and who all these strange humans are. It's best to let him explore on his own and meet the family members as he feels comfortable. Let him investigate all the new smells, sights and sounds at his own pace. Children should be especially careful to not get overly excited, use loud voices or hug the pup too tightly. Be calm, gentle and affectionate, and be ready to comfort him if he appears frightened or uneasy.

Be sure to show your puppy his new crate during this first day home. Toss a treat or two inside the crate; if he associates the crate with food, he will associate the crate with good things. If he is comfortable with the crate, you can offer him his first meal inside it. Leave the door ajar so he can wander in and out as he chooses.

A pile of snuggling Leo littermates. Your pup will miss the warmth of his brothers and sisters when you first bring him home.

WATCH THE WATER

To help your puppy sleep through the night without having to relieve himself, remove his water bowl after 7 p.m. Offer him a couple of ice cubes during the evening to quench his thirst. Never leave water in a puppy's crate, as this is inviting puddles of mishaps.

FIRST NIGHT IN HIS NEW HOME

So much has happened in your Leonberger puppy's first day away from the breeder. He's had his first car ride to his new home. He's met his new human family and perhaps the other family pets. He has explored his new house and yard, at least those places where he is to be allowed during his first weeks at home. He may have visited his new veterinarian. He has eaten his first meal or two away from his dam and litter-mates. Surely that's enough to tire out an eight-week-old Leonberger pup…or so you hope!

It's bedtime. During the day, the pup investigated his crate, which is his new den and sleeping space, so it is not entirely strange to him. Line the crate with a soft towel or blanket that he can snuggle into and gently place him into the crate for the night. Some breeders send home a piece of bedding from where the pup slept with his littermates, and those familiar scents are a great comfort for the puppy on his first night without his siblings.

He will probably whine or cry. The puppy is objecting to the confinement and the fact that he is alone for the first time. This can be a stressful time for you as well as for the pup. It's important that you remain strong and don't let the puppy out of his crate to comfort him. He will fall asleep eventually. If you release him, the puppy will learn that crying means "out" and will continue that habit. You are laying the groundwork for future habits. Some breeders find that soft music can soothe a crying pup and help him get to sleep.

SOCIALIZING YOUR PUPPY

The first 20 weeks of your Leonberger puppy's life are the most important of his entire lifetime. A properly socialized puppy will grow up to be a

A sturdy chew will keep puppy teeth busy and puppy owners happy!

**Puppy pals!
Socialization is
essential;
fortunately, Leo
pups are naturally
friendly creatures
who enjoy
meeting all kinds
of acquaintances.**

confident and stable adult who will be a pleasure to live with and a welcome addition to the neighborhood.

The importance of socialization cannot be overemphasized. Research on canine behavior has proven that puppies who are not exposed to new sights, sounds, people and animals during their first 20 weeks of life will grow up to be timid and fearful, even aggressive, and unable to flourish outside of their familiar home environment. You want your dog to be friendly and reliable around all people and animals and in all situations.

Socializing your puppy is not difficult and, in fact, will be a fun time for you both. Lead training goes hand in hand with socialization, so your puppy will be learning how to walk on a lead at the same time that he's meeting the neighborhood. Because the Leonberger is such a terrific breed, your puppy will enjoy being "the new kid on the block" that

everyone wants to meet. Take him for short walks, to the park and to other dog-friendly places where he will encounter new people, especially children. Puppies automatically recognize children as "little people" and are drawn to play with them. Just make sure that you supervise these meetings and that the children do not get too rough or encourage him to play too hard. An overzealous pup can often nip too hard, frightening the child and in turn making the puppy overly excited. A bad experience in puppyhood can impact a dog for life, so a pup that has a negative experience with a child may grow up to be shy or even aggressive around children.

Take your puppy along on your daily errands. Puppies are natural "people magnets," and most people who see your pup will want to pet him. All of these encounters will help to mold him into a confident adult dog. Likewise, you will soon feel like a confident, responsible dog owner, rightly proud of your mannerly Leonberger.

Be especially careful of your puppy's encounters and experiences during the eight-to-ten-week-old period, which is also called the "fear period." This is a serious imprinting period, and all contact during this time should be gentle and positive. A frightening or negative event could leave a

CREATE A SCHEDULE

Puppies thrive on sameness and routine. Offer meals at the same time each day, take him out at regular times for potty trips and do the same for play periods and outdoor activity. Make note of when your puppy naps and when he is most lively and energetic, and try to plan his day around those times. Once he is house-trained and more predictable in his habits, he will be better able to tolerate changes in his schedule.

permanent impression that could affect his future behavior if a similar situation arises.

Also make sure that your puppy has received his first and second rounds of vaccinations before you expose him to other dogs or bring him to places that other dogs may frequent. Avoid dog parks and other strange-dog areas until your vet assures you that your puppy is fully immunized and resistant to the diseases that can be passed

between canines. Discuss socialization with your breeder, as some breeders recommend socializing the puppy even before he has received all of his inoculations, depending on how outgoing the puppy may be.

SOLVING PUPPY PROBLEMS

CHEWING AND NIPPING

Nipping at fingers and toes is normal puppy behavior. Chewing is also the way that puppies investigate their surroundings. However, you will have to dedicate yourself to teaching your puppy that chewing anything other than his toys is not acceptable. That won't happen overnight and at times your Leo's teeth will test your patience. However, if you allow nipping and chewing to continue, just think about the damage that a mature Leonberger can do with a full set of adult teeth.

Whenever your puppy nips your hand or fingers, cry out

Who's going to be "top pup"? Puppies learn to be part of a pack by roughhousing with their littermates and playfully posturing for position.

THE FAMILY FELINE

A resident cat has feline squatter's rights. The cat will treat the newcomer (your puppy) as she sees fit, regardless of what you do or say. So it's best to let the two of them work things out on their own terms. Cats have a height advantage and will generally leap to higher ground to avoid direct contact with a rambunctious pup. Some will hiss and boldly swat at a pup who passes by or tries to reach the cat. Keep the puppy under control in the presence of the cat and they will eventually become accustomed to each other.

Here's a hint: move the cat's litter box where the puppy can't get into it! It's best to do so well before the pup comes home so the cat is used to the new location.

"Ouch!" in a loud voice, which should startle your puppy and stop him from nipping, even if only for a moment. Immediately distract him by offering a small treat or an appropriate toy for him to chew instead (which means having chew toys and puppy treats handy or in your pockets at all times). Praise him when he takes the toy and tell him what a good fellow he is. Praise is just as or even more important in puppy training as discipline and correction.

Puppies also tend to nip at children more often than adults, since they perceive little ones to be more vulnerable and more similar to their littermates. Teach your children appropriate responses to nipping behavior. If they are unable to handle it themselves, you may have to intervene. Puppy nips can be quite painful, and a child's frightened reaction will only encourage a puppy to nip harder, which is a natural canine response. As with all other puppy situations, interaction between your Leonberger puppy and children should be supervised.

Chewing on objects, not just family members' fingers and ankles, is also normal canine behavior that can be especially tedious (for the owner, not the pup) during the teething period when the puppy's adult teeth are coming in. At this stage, chewing just plain feels good. Furniture legs and cabinet corners are common puppy favorites. Shoes and other personal items also taste pretty good to a pup.

The best solution is, once again, prevention. If you value something, keep it tucked away and out of reach. You can't hide your dining-room table in a closet, but you can try to deflect the chewing by applying a bitter product made just to deter dogs from chewing. Available in a spray or cream, this substance is vile-tasting, although safe for dogs, and most puppies will avoid the forbidden object after one tiny taste. You also can apply the product to your leather leash if the puppy tries to chew on his lead during leash-training sessions.

Keep a ready supply of safe chews handy to offer your Leonberger as a distraction when he starts to chew on something that's a "no-no." Remember, at this tender age he does not yet know what is permitted or forbidden, so you have to be "on call" every minute he's awake and on the prowl.

You may lose a treasure or two during puppy's growing-up period, and the furniture could sustain a nasty nick or two. These can be trying times, so be prepared for those inevitable accidents and try to stay one step ahead of your Leo.

JUMPING UP

Leo puppies jump up...on you, your guests, your counters and your furniture. Just another normal part of growing up, and one you need to meet head-on if you want to stop it from becoming a habit. If not taught otherwise, your adult Leo will find this a perfectly acceptable way to greet you and everyone else.

The key to jump correction is consistency. You cannot correct your Leonberger for jumping up on you today, then allow it to happen tomorrow by greeting him with hugs and kisses. As you have learned by now, consistency is critical to all puppy lessons.

For starters, try turning your back as soon as the puppy jumps. Jumping up is a means of gaining your attention and, if the pup can't see your face, he may get discouraged and learn that he

Winnie, a Leo youngster pictured at 13 weeks old.

loses eye contact with his beloved master when he jumps up.

Leash corrections also work, and most puppies respond well to a leash tug if they jump. Grasp the leash close to the puppy's collar and give a quick tug downward, using the command "Off." Do not use the word "Down," since "Down" is used to teach the puppy to lie down, which is a separate action that he will learn during his education in the basic commands. As soon as the puppy has backed off, tell him to sit and immediately praise him for doing so. This will take many repetitions and won't be accomplished quickly, so don't get discouraged or give up; you must be even more persistent than your puppy.

A second method used for jump correction is the spritzer bottle. Fill a spray bottle with water mixed with a bit of lemon juice or vinegar. As soon as puppy jumps, command him "Off" and spritz him with the water mixture. Of course, that means having the spray bottle handy whenever or wherever jumping usually happens.

Yet a third method to discourage jumping is grasping the puppy's paws and holding them gently but firmly until he struggles to get away. Wait a brief moment or two, then release his paws and give him a command to sit. He should eventually learn that jumping gets him into an uncomfortable predicament.

Children are major victims of puppy jumping, since puppies view little people as ready targets for jumping up as well as nipping. If your children (or their friends) are unable to dispense jump corrections, you will have to intervene and handle it for them.

Important to prevention is also knowing what you should *not* do. Never kick your Leo (for any reason, not just for jumping) or knock him in the chest with your knee. That maneuver could actually harm your puppy. Vets can tell you stories about puppies who suffered broken bones after being banged about when they jumped up.

PUPPY WHINING

Puppies often cry and whine, just as infants and little children do. It's their way of telling us that they are lonely or in need of attention. Your puppy will miss his littermates and will feel insecure when he is left alone. You may be out of the house or

TASTY LESSONS

The best route to teaching a very young puppy is through his tummy. Use tiny bits of soft puppy treats to teach obedience commands like come, sit and down. Don't overdo treats; schooltime is not meant to be mealtime.

A well-bred Leo puppy is a true gift that will become a real part of the family. This is Stormchaser Shooting Star at four weeks of age.

just in another room, but he will still feel alone. During these times, the puppy's crate should be his personal comfort station, a place all his own where he can feel safe and secure. Once he learns that being alone is okay and not something to be feared, he will settle down without crying or objecting. Teaching the Leo pup that "alone" is "okay" will take some commitment, because he truly hates being alone, constantly craving human attention. You might want to leave a radio on while he is crated, as the sound of human voices can be soothing and will give the impression that people are around. Also give your puppy a favorite sturdy chew toy to entertain him whenever he is crated. You will both be happier: the puppy because he is safe in his den and you because he is quiet, safe and not getting into puppy escapades that can wreak havoc in your house or cause him danger.

To make sure that your puppy will always view his crate as a safe and cozy place, never, *ever*, use the crate as punishment. That's the best way to turn the crate into a negative place that the pup will want to avoid. Sure, you can use the crate for your own peace of mind if your puppy is getting into trouble and needs some "time out." Just don't let him know that! Never scold the pup and immediately place him into the crate. Count to ten, give him a couple of hugs and maybe a treat, then scoot him into his crate.

It's also important not to make a big fuss when he is released from the crate. That will make getting out of the crate more appealing than being in the crate, which is just the opposite of what you are trying to achieve.

PROPER CARE OF YOUR

LEONBERGER

Adding a Leonberger to your household means adding a new family member who will need your care each and every day. When your Leonberger pup first comes home, you will start a routine with him so that, as he grows up, your dog will have a daily schedule just as you do. The aspects of your dog's daily care will likewise become regular parts of your day, so you'll both have a new schedule. Dogs learn by consistency and thrive on routine: regular times for meals, exercise, grooming and potty trips are just as important for your dog as they are to you! Your dog's schedule will depend much on your family's daily routine, but remember that you now have a new member of the family who is part of your day every day.

FEEDING THE LEONBERGER
In general, there are no particular dietary problems in Leonbergers and, therefore, feeding is much the same as with all other breeds. The dog needs a well-balanced diet and the easiest way to achieve this is by feeding a dry complete food. There are many brands on the market, ranging in price and quality. They vary in ingredients—chicken, lamb, fish and even vegetables. What is important is that the dog enjoys his meals, that the food gives the dog energy, stamina and a glossy coat and that he is healthy and able to enjoy life.

When buying a new puppy, the breeder should give you a diet sheet that details the puppy's daily menu. It is best to stay with the same food, at least for a while. Settling into a new home must be quite traumatic, so feeding him his familiar food should help somewhat.

An eight-week-old puppy is capable of eating dry food, either moistened with water or with a bit of canned food mixed in. Start off with feeding a puppy food, which is generally higher in protein than adult food and smaller in kibble size. However, be careful and avoid a puppy food too high in protein, as we need our Leonbergers to grow slowly. If they grow too quickly, they may suffer lameness caused by panosteitis, a hereditary and inflammatory condition that affects the leg bones of puppies under a year old.

By the time your puppy is six months old, he will need a larger-kibble food. Most manufacturers produce a junior diet and many make kibble suitable for giant breeds. An adult diet should be quite sufficient to sustain him at 18 months old. Mixing in a little bit of canned food is a good bloat-preventive while preserving the dental benefits of the crunchy food.

Every package of food has a list of ingredients, so you can check to see if the food contains anything that does not agree with your dog. Also on the bag are guidelines of how much to feed him.

There are other methods of feeding dogs. A meat and biscuit diet is one way, but should you decide to feed this diet, you will need to add supplements, especially through puppyhood. Calcium and multi-vitamin tablets will help make this method a balanced diet. The guidelines for the amount of tablets to be given are on the packaging, but you should definitely seek the advice of your vet before attempting to feed a diet you make yourself. Instead of meat, you may like to feed tripe, which is a popular alternative embraced by many owners. Owners should be aware that certain "people foods" are toxic to dogs. These include chocolate, onions, grapes, raisins and nuts. Keep this in mind when

WEIGHT AND SEE!

When you look at yourself in the mirror each day, you get very used to what you see! It's only when you pull out last year's vacation outfit and can't zip it up that you notice that you've put on some pounds. Dog owners are the same way with their dogs. Often a few pounds go unnoticed, and it's not until some time passes or the vet remarks that your dog looks more than pleasantly plump that you realize what's happened. To avoid your pet's becoming obese right under your very nose, make a habit of routinely evaluating his condition with a hands-on test.

Can you feel, but not see, your dog's rib cage? Does your dog have a waist? His waist should be evident by touch and also visible from above and from the side. In top view, the dog's body should have an hourglass shape. These are indicators of good condition. With a heavily-coated breed, it's easier to feel than see.

While it's not hard to spot an extremely skinny or overly rotund dog, it's the subtle changes that lead up to under- or overweight condition of which we must be aware. If your dog's ribs are visible, he is too thin. Conversely, if you can't feel the ribs under too much fat, and if there's no indication of a waistline, your dog is overweight. Both of these conditions require changes to the diet. A trip or sometimes just a call to the vet will help you modify your dog's feeding.

Your breeder's knowledge of the breed and healthy growth helps him start the pups off on a diet with optimal nutrition.

WATER

Every Leo's favorite topic—H_2O! Just as your dog needs proper nutrition from his food, water is an essential "nutrient" as well. Water keeps the dog's body properly hydrated and promotes normal function of the body's systems. During house-training, it is necessary to keep an eye on how much water your Leonberger is drinking, but once he is reliably

your Leo is gazing at you longingly for a taste of your meal.

It is recommended that you feed your adult Leonberger at least twice a day, his daily ration being divided into two or even three meals. Large, deep-chested dogs can suffer from bloat (torsion), in which the stomach twists. If not detected immediately, the consequences of bloat can be tragic. Your dog should not partake of any vigorous exercise for at least two hours before or after a meal. He should be encouraged to lie down and rest before and after meals.

Don't forget the water, especially when spending time outdoors in warm weather.

SWITCHING FOODS

There are certain times in a dog's life when it becomes necessary to switch his food; for example, from puppy to adult food and then from adult to senior-dog food. Additionally, you may decide to feed your pup a different type of food from what he received from the breeder, and there may be "emergency" situations in which you can't find your dog's normal brand and have to offer something else temporarily. Anytime a change is made, for whatever reason, the switch must be done gradually. You don't want to upset the dog's stomach or end up with a picky eater who refuses to eat something new. A tried-and-true approach is, over the course of about a week, to mix a little of the new food in with the old, increasing the proportion of new to old as the days progress. At the end of the week, you'll be feeding his regular portions of the new food, and he will barely notice the change.

What Is "Bloat"?

Need yet another reason to avoid tossing your dog a morsel from your plate? It is shown that dogs fed table scraps have an increased risk of developing bloat, or (gastric torsion). Did you know that more occurrences of bloat occur in the warm-weather months due to the frequency of outdoor cooking and dining and dogs' receiving "samples" from the fired-up grill?

You likely have heard the term "bloat," which refers to gastric torsion (gastric dilatation/volvulus), a potentially fatal condition. As it is directly related to feeding and exercise practices, a brief explanation here is warranted. The term *dilatation* means that the dog's stomach is filled with air, while *volvulus* means that the stomach is twisted around on itself, blocking the entrance/exit points. Dilatation/volvulus is truly a deadly combination, although they also can occur independently of each other. An affected dog cannot digest food or pass gas, and blood cannot flow to the stomach, causing accumulation of toxins and gas along with great pain and rapidly occuring shock.

Many theories exist on what exactly causes bloat, but we do know that deep-chested breeds are more prone. Activities like eating a large meal, gulping water, strenuous exercise too close to mealtimes or a combination of these factors can contribute to bloat, though not every case is directly related to these more well-known causes. With that in mind, we can focus on incorporating simple daily preventives and knowing how to recognize the symptoms; in addition to tips mentioned in this book, your vet can advise you about how to prevent bloat and recognize the symptoms. Affected dogs need immediate veterinary attention, as death can result quickly. Signs include obvious restlessness/discomfort, crying in pain, drooling/excessive salivation, unproductive attempts to vomit or relieve himself, visibly bloated appearance and collapsing. Do not wait—get to the vet *right away* if you see any of these symptoms. The vet will confirm by x-ray if the stomach is bloated with air; if so, the dog must be treated *immediately*.

A bloated dog will be treated for shock, and the stomach must be relieved of the air pressure as well as surgically returned to its correct position. If part of the stomach wall has died, that part must be removed. Usually the stomach is stapled to the abdominal wall to prevent another episode of bloating; this may or may not be successful. The vet should also check the dog for heart problems, which can be side effects of bloat. As you can see, it's much easier and safer to prevent bloat than to treat it.

Dig in! The Leonberger approaches everything he does with gusto, including dinner.

trained he should have ready access to clean fresh water. As a bloat preventive, water should be restricted at mealtimes and your Leo should never be allowed to gulp his water (or food). Make certain that the dog's water bowl is clean, and change (and *refill*) the water often. Your Leo will "use" more water than most dogs, whether drinking, splashing or bathing.

BLOAT-PREVENTION TIPS

As varied as the causes of bloat are the tips for prevention, but some common preventive methods follow:

- Feed two or three small meals daily rather than one large one;

- Do not feed water before, after or with meals, but allow access to water at all other times;

- Never permit rapid eating or gulping of water;

- No exercise for the dog at least two hours before and (especially) after meals;

- Feed high-quality food with adequate protein, adequate fiber content and not too much fat and carbohydrate;

- Explore herbal additives, enzymes or gas-reduction products (only under a vet's advice) to encourage a "friendly" environment in the dog's digestive system;

- Avoid foods and ingredients known to produce gas;

- Avoid stressful situations for the dog, especially at mealtimes;

- Make dietary changes gradually, over a period of a few weeks;

- Do not feed dry food only;

- Although the role of genetics as a causative of bloat is not known, many breeders do not breed from previously affected dogs;

- Sometimes owners are advised to have gastro-plexy (stomach stapling) performed on their dogs as a preventive measure.

Of utmost importance is that you know your dog! Pay attention to his behavior and any changes that could be symptomatic of bloat. Your dog's life depends on it!

EXERCISE

The adult Leonberger requires approximately two half-hour walks per day, though should you want to give him more, he will certainly be only too happy to accept. Exercising a puppy has to be done with caution, especially any vigorous activity that could cause stress to the Leo's growing bones, such as stair climbing or chasing a toy around the yard. Puppies' bones are soft and too much of the wrong exercise can do untold damage.

Young puppies should not be walked for miles on the end of a lead, as they cannot lie down and rest when they are tired. Give them just gentle walks, about 200 or so yards to start with at about 12 weeks old, and gradually increase the distance as the pup gets older. The puppy will probably get enough exercise in his first three months just playing around the home, but never allow him to climb the stairs; also, never let a puppy run free with adult dogs.

Leonbergers are agile dogs and, in general, good swimmers. Many belong to agility clubs and flyball clubs, and though they may not be able to keep up with dogs like the Border Collie, it is fun and good exercise for dog and handler. Some Newfoundland water-trial clubs will allow Leonbergers to join, and this sport is one in which the Leonberger can really

FEEDING IN HOT WEATHER

Even the most dedicated chow hound may have less of an appetite when the weather is hot or humid. If your dog leaves more of his food behind than usual, adjust his portions until the weather and his appetite return to normal. Never leave the uneaten portion in the bowl, hoping he will return to finish it, because higher temperatures encourage food spoilage and bacterial growth.

excel. To witness a dog pull in a boat or a person is a wonderful sight, but just swimming with your dog is an experience in itself.

GROOMING

ROUTINE MAINTENANCE

The Leonberger has quite a substantial coat of two layers, a soft pale cream undercoat and a coarser top coat. He has an abundance of hair on his ears, on all four legs and around his neck. To keep the coat clean, you must brush the dog regularly. About twice a year, the Leonberger sheds and the undercoat falls away, leaving just the coarser hair. Constant brushing and combing is important at these times to remove any knots and mats that may develop. Shedding times also afford ideal opportunities to check for any lumps or skin infections, as it is easier to see through the hair.

The hair behind and below the ears will knot often, which can be caused by a waxy discharge or the

A COAT IN THE SUMMER

A dog's long or heavy coat is designed for insulation in any type of weather, so think again before giving your dog a summer haircut. Shaving down his coat in warm weather will affect his body's natural temperature regulation and is neither necessary nor beneficial.

dog's scratching. Clean inside the ears with a soft cotton ball or pad and an ear cleanser, and comb out any knots. The longer hair on the legs and neck needs more attention than that on the rest of the body because, like that on the ears, it becomes tangled easily. The best tool for this is a rake with rotating teeth. It is less likely to hurt the dog when pulling at delicate skin.

The feet need trimming at regular intervals, as the hair grows constantly between the toes and pads. Trim the feet so that the hair looks the same length all over, and check between the toes for mats and comb out.

Teeth also need cleaning, and it is a good idea to get the young puppy used to this as soon as possible. Puppies may not like having their teeth brushed during teething, but once the adult teeth have come in, cleaning is a must to keep the gums healthy and the teeth white. Toothpaste

Spot cleanings may be necessary between baths if your Leo likes to get his paws dirty.

Water is essential for Leonbergers of all ages, although it's typical of Leo pups that they would rather have a splash than have a drink!

A rake is a helpful grooming tool for maintaining the Leo's coat, which is abundant all over the body.

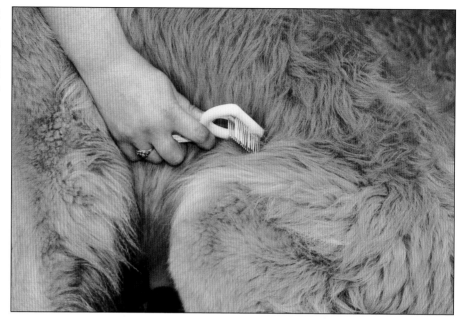

formulated for dogs can be obtained from your vet or pet shop (do not use human toothpaste). Together with a doggy toothbrush or your finger, apply paste to the teeth inside and out. Some toothpastes can be put in the dog's food.

Your local pet shop will have a variety of grooming items that will assist you in keeping your Leonberger's coat in proper condition.

Always check under your dog's tail regularly. Infections, such as an abscess or impacted glands, can build up around the anus in a very short time. These need veterinary treatment as soon as they are spotted.

Add to your grooming routine a wipe around the dog's eyes with a soft tissue to remove any matter; if done on a daily basis, your dog should look in top condition.

NAIL CLIPPING

Having his nails trimmed is not on many dogs' lists of favorite things to do. With this in mind, you will need to accustom your puppy to the procedure at a young age so that he will sit still (well, as still as he can) for his pedicures. Long nails can cause the dog's feet to spread, which is not good for him; likewise, long nails can hurt if they unintentionally scratch, not good for you!

Some dogs' nails are worn down naturally by regular walking on hard surfaces, so the frequency with which you clip depends on your individual dog. Look at his nails from time to time and clip as needed; a good way to know when it's time for a trim is if you hear your dog clicking as he walks across the floor.

There are several types of nail clippers and even electric nail-grinding tools made for dogs; first we'll discuss using the clipper. To start, have your clipper ready and

THE EARS KNOW

Examining your puppy's ears helps ensure good internal health. The ears are the eyes to the dog's innards! Begin handling your puppy's ears when he's still young so that he doesn't protest every time you lift a flap or touch his ears. Yeast and bacteria are two of the culprits that you can detect by examining the ear. You will notice a strong, often foul, odor, debris, redness or some kind of discharge. All of these point to health problems that can worsen over time. Additionally, you are on the lookout for wax accumulation, ear mites and other tiny bothersome parasites and their even tinier droppings. You may have to pluck hair with tweezers in order to have a better view into the dog's ears, but this is painless if done carefully. Make cleaning your Leo's ears part of your grooming routine. Weekly cleaning with soft cotton and an ear-cleaning powder or liquid should keep healthy ears clean.

some doggie treats on hand. You want your pup to view his nail-clipping sessions in a positive

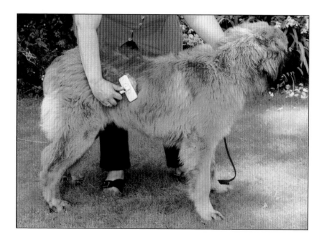

The Leo's coat sheds twice a year, requiring daily attention until the soft undercoat has completely been shed.

A heavy-duty nail clipper designed for use on canines will be necessary for clipping your Leo's nails.

blades on the top and bottom snip it off in one clip.

Start by grasping the pup's paw; a little pressure on the foot pad causes the nail to extend, making it easier to clip. Clip off a little at a time. If you can see the "quick," which is a blood vessel that runs through each nail, you will know how much to trim, as you do not want to cut into the quick. On that note, if you do cut the quick, which will cause bleeding, you can stem the flow of blood with a styptic pencil or other clotting agent. If you mistakenly nip the quick, do not panic or fuss, as this will cause the pup to be afraid. Simply reassure the pup, stop the bleeding and move on to the next nail. Don't be discouraged; you will become a professional canine pedicurist with practice.

You may or may not be able to see the quick, so it's best to just clip off a small bit at a time. If you see a dark dot in the center of the nail, this is the quick and your cue to stop clipping. Tell the puppy he's a "good boy" and offer a piece of treat with each nail. You can also use nail-clipping time to examine the footpads, making sure that they are not dry and cracked and that nothing has become embedded in them.

The nail grinder, the other choice, is many owners' first choice. Accustoming the puppy to the sound of the grinder and

light, and what better way to convince him than with food? You may want to enlist the help of an assistant to comfort the pup and offer treats as you concentrate on the clipping itself. The guillotine-type clipper is thought of by many as the easiest type to use; the nail tip is inserted into the opening, and

You must take care of your Leo's teeth. He'll thank you for it!

to be bathed nearly as often as humans, but regular bathing is essential for healthy skin and a healthy, shiny coat.

In general, dogs need to be bathed only a few times a year, possibly more often if your dog gets into something messy or if he starts to smell like a dog. Show dogs are usually bathed before every show, which could be as frequent as weekly, although this depends on the owner and the dog. Bathing too frequently can have negative effects on the skin and coat, removing natural oils and causing dryness.

You may also need to bathe your Leo after a swim, whether that dip is a planned visit to the lake or an improvisational roll in a mud puddle. Leos don't mind the wet stuff, but don't bathe him too often.

When it's time for a bath, it shouldn't take much coaxing to convince a water-loving Leo to get into the tub.

sensation of the buzz presents fewer challenges than the clipper, and there's no chance of cutting through the quick. Use the grinder on a low setting and always talk soothingly to your dog. He won't mind his salon visit, and he'll have nicely polished nails as well.

BATHING

Few dogs enjoy a bath as much as the Leonberger—a fortunate blessing since bathing an unwilling Leonberger would be no easy chore. Dogs do not need

SCOOTING HIS BOTTOM

Here's a doggy problem that many owners tend to neglect. If your dog is scooting his rear end around the carpet, he probably is experiencing anal-sac impaction or blockage. The anal sacs are the two grape-sized glands on either side of the dog's vent. The dog cannot empty these glands, which become filled with a foul-smelling material. The dog may attempt to lick the area to relieve the pressure. He may also rub his anus on your walls, furniture or floors.

Don't neglect your dog's rear end during grooming sessions. By squeezing both sides of the anus with a soft cloth, you can express some of the material in the sacs. If the material is pasty and thick, you likely will need the assistance of a veterinarian. Vets know how to express the glands and can show you how to do it correctly without hurting the dog or spraying yourself with the unpleasant liquid.

To complicate matters, Leos can be affected by perianal fistulas. These are thought to be inherited in the breed; they appear like infected anal sacs but are more serious and difficult to treat, requiring veterinary aid.

Before bathing the dog, have the items you'll need close at hand. First, decide where you will bathe the dog. You should have a tub or large basin with a non-slip surface. In warm weather, some like to use a portable pool in the yard, although you'll want to make sure your dog doesn't head for the nearest dirt pile following his bath! You will also need a hose or shower spray to wet the coat thoroughly, a shampoo formulated for dogs, absorbent towels and a blow dryer, either one made for drying dogs or your own on low heat. Human shampoos are too harsh for dogs' coats and will dry them out.

Before wetting the dog, give him a brush-through to remove any dead hair, dirt and mats. Make sure he is at ease in the tub and have the water at a comfortable temperature. Begin bathing by wetting the coat all the way down to the skin. Massage in the shampoo, keeping it away from his face and eyes. Rinse him thoroughly, again avoiding the eyes and ears, as you don't want to get water into the ear canals. A thorough rinsing is important, as shampoo residue is drying and itchy to the dog. After rinsing, wrap him in a towel to absorb the initial moisture. You can finish drying with either a towel or a blow dryer on low heat, held at a safe distance from the dog. You should keep the dog indoors and away from drafts until he is completely dry.

EYE CARE

During grooming sessions, pay extra attention to the condition of your dog's eyes. If the area around the eyes is soiled or if tear staining has occurred, there are various cleaning agents made especially for this purpose. Look at the dog's eyes to make sure no debris has entered; dogs with large eyes and those who spend time outdoors are especially prone to this.

The signs of an eye infection are obvious: mucus, redness, puffiness, scabs or other signs of irritation. If your dog's eyes become infected, the vet will likely prescribe an antibiotic ointment for treatment. If you notice signs of more serious problems, such as opacities in the eye, which usually indicate cataracts, consult the vet at once. Taking time to pay attention to your dog's eyes will alert you in the early stages of any problem so that you can get your dog treatment as soon as possible. You could save your dog's sight!

IDENTIFICATION AND TRAVEL

ID FOR YOUR DOG

You love your Leonberger and want to keep him safe. Of course, you take every precaution to prevent his escaping from the yard or becoming lost or stolen. You have a sturdy high fence and you always keep your dog on lead when out and about in public places. If your dog is not properly identified, however, you are overlooking a major aspect of his safety. We hope to never be in a situation where our dog is missing, but we should practice prevention in the unfortunate case that this happens; identification greatly increases the chances of your dog's being returned to you

There are several ways to identify your dog. First, the traditional dog tag should be a staple in your dog's wardrobe, attached to his everyday collar. Tags can be made of sturdy plastic and various metals and should include your contact information so that a person who finds the dog can get in touch with you right away to arrange his return. Many people today enjoy the wide range of decorative tags available, so have fun and create a tag to match your dog's personality. Of course, it is important that the tag stays

PET OR STRAY?

Besides the obvious benefit of providing your contact information to whoever finds your lost dog, an ID tag makes your dog more approachable and more likely to be recovered. A strange dog wandering the neighborhood without a collar and tags will look like a stray, while the collar and tags indicate that the dog is someone's pet. Even if the ID tags become detached from the collar, the collar alone will make a person more likely to pick up the dog.

Transporting a large dog requires a large vehicle. If there isn't enough space for your Leo's crate, a partition across the back of the vehicle is an option for safe travel.

on the collar, so have a secure "O" ring attachment; you also can explore the type of tag that slides right onto the collar.

In addition to the ID tag, which every dog should wear even if identified by another method, two other forms of identification have become popular: microchipping and tattooing. In microchipping, a tiny scannable chip is painlessly inserted under the dog's skin. The number is registered to you so that, if your lost dog turns up at a clinic or shelter, the chip can be scanned to retrieve your contact information.

The advantage of the microchip is that it is a permanent form of ID, but there are some factors to consider. Several different companies make microchips, and not all are compatible with the others' scanning devices. It's best to find a company with a universal

microchip that can be read by scanners made by other companies as well. It won't do any good to have the dog chipped if the information cannot be retrieved. Also, not every humane society, shelter and clinic is equipped with a scanner, although more and more facilities are equipping themselves. In fact, many shelters microchip dogs that they adopt out to new homes.

In the US, there are five or six major microchip manufacturers as well as a few databases. The American Kennel Club's Companion Animal Recovery unit works in conjunction with HomeAgain™ Companion Animal Retrieval System (Schering-Plough). In the UK, The Kennel Club is affiliated with the National Pet Register, operated by Wood Green Animal Shelters.

Because the microchip is not visible to the eye, the dog must wear a tag that states that he is microchipped so that whoever picks him up will know to have him scanned. He of course also should have a tag with contact information in case his chip cannot be read. Humane societies and veterinary clinics offer microchipping service, which is usually very affordable.

Though less popular than microchipping, tattooing is another permanent method of ID for dogs. Most vets perform this service, and there are also clinics that perform dog tattooing. This is also an affordable procedure and one that will not cause much discomfort for the dog. It is best to put the tattoo in a visible area, such as the ear, to deter theft. It is sad to say that there are cases of dogs' being stolen and sold to research laboratories, but such laboratories will not accept tattooed dogs.

To ensure that the tattoo is effective in aiding your dog's return to you, the tattoo number must be registered with a national organization. That way, when someone finds a tattooed dog, a phone call to the registry will quickly match the dog with his owner.

HIT THE ROAD

Car travel with your Leonberger may be limited to necessity only, such as trips to the vet, or you may bring your dog along almost everywhere you go. This will depend much on your individual dog and how he reacts to rides in the car. You can begin desensitizing your dog to car travel as a pup so that it's something that he's used to. Still, some dogs suffer from motion sickness. Your vet may prescribe a medication for this if trips in the car pose a problem for your dog. At the very least, you will need to get him to the vet, so he will need to tolerate these trips with the least amount of hassle possible.

Start taking your pup on short trips, maybe just around the block to start. If he is fine with short trips, lengthen your rides a little at a time. Start to take him on your errands or just for drives around town. By this time, it will be easy to tell whether your dog is a born traveler or would prefer staying at home when you are on the road.

Of course, safety is a concern for dogs in the car. First, he must

Your Leo's leash and collar are travel essentials.

Traveling in comfort, this Leo has a safely partitioned area of the car just for him.

travel securely, not left loose to roam about the car where he could be injured or distract the driver. A young pup can be held by a passenger initially but will quickly beome too large to be held. He should soon graduate to a travel crate, which can be the same crate he uses in the home provided your vehicle is large enough to accommodate the Leo's large crate. Other options include a car harness (like a seat belt for dogs) and partitioning the back of the car with a gate made for this purpose.

Bring along what you will need for the dog. He should wear his collar and ID tags, of course, and you should bring his leash, water (and food if a long trip) and clean-up materials for potty breaks and in case of motion sickness. Always keep your dog on his leash when you make stops, and never leave him alone in the car. Many a dog has died from the heat inside a closed car; this does not take much time at all in any kind of weather. A dog left alone inside a car can also be a target for thieves.

BOARDING

Today there are many options for dog owners who need someone to care for their dogs in certain circumstances. While many think of boarding their dogs as something to do when away on vacation, many others use the services of doggie "daycare" facilities, dropping their dogs off to spend the day while they are at work. Many of these facilities offer both long-term and daily care. Many go beyond just boarding and

DOGGONE!
Wendy Ballard is the editor and publisher of the *DogGone*™ newsletter, which comes out bi-monthly and features fun articles by dog owners who love to travel with their dogs. The newsletter includes information about fun places to go with your dogs, including popular vacation spots, dog-friendly hotels, parks, campgrounds, resorts, etc., as well as interesting activities to do with your dog, such as flyball, agility and much more. You can subscribe to the publication by contacting the publisher at PO Box 651155, Vero Beach, FL 32965-1155.

cater to all sorts of needs, with on-site grooming, veterinary care, training classes and even "web-cams" where owners can log on to the Internet and check out what their dogs are up to. Most dogs enjoy the activity and time spent with other dogs.

Before you need to use such a service, check out the ones in your area. Make visits to see the facilities, meet the staff, discuss fees and available services and see whether this is a place where you think your dog will be happy. Do they have experience with giant breeds and enough space to comfortably house your Leo? It is best to do your research in advance so that you're not stuck at the last minute,

forced into making a rushed decision without knowing whether the kennel that you've chosen meets your standards. You also can check with your vet's office to see whether they offer boarding for their clients or can recommend a good kennel in the area.

The kennel will need to see proof of your dog's health records and vaccinations so as not to spread illness from dog to dog. Your dog also will need proper identification. Owners usually experience some separation anxiety the first time they have to leave their dog in someone else's care, so it's reassuring to know that the kennel you choose is run by experienced, caring dog people.

Visit boarding kennels in your area so that you know you will be comfortable leaving your dog in the care of the facility that you choose. Be certain they accept large dogs.

LEONBERGER

BASIC TRAINING PRINCIPLES: PUPPY VS. ADULT

There's a big difference between training an adult dog and training a young puppy. With a young puppy, everything is new. At eight to ten weeks of age, he will be experiencing many things, and he has nothing with which to compare these experiences. Up to this point, he has been with his dam and littermates, not one-on-one with people except in his interactions with his breeder and visitors to the litter.

When you first bring the puppy home, he is eager to please you. This means that he accepts doing things your way. During the next couple of months, he will absorb the basis of everything he needs to know for the rest of his life. This early age is even referred to as the "sponge" stage. After that, for the next 18 months, it's up to you to reinforce good manners by building on the foundation that you've established. Once your puppy is reliable in basic commands and behavior and has reached the appropriate age, you may gradually introduce him to some

LEADER OF THE PACK

Canines are pack animals. They live according to pack rules, and every pack has only one leader. Guess what? That's you! To establish your position of authority, lay down the rules and be fair and good-natured in all your dealings with your dog. He will consider young children as his littermates, but the one who trains him, who feeds him, who grooms him, who expects him to come into line, that's his leader. And he who leads must be obeyed.

of the interesting sports, games and activities available to pet owners and their dogs.

Raising your puppy is a family affair. Each member of the family must know what rules to set forth for the puppy and how to use the same one-word commands to mean exactly the same thing every time. Even if yours is a large family, one person will soon be considered by the pup to be the leader, the Alpha person in his pack, the "boss" who must be obeyed. Often that highly regarded person turns out to be the one who feeds the puppy. Food ranks very high on the puppy's list of important things! That's why your puppy is rewarded with small treats along with verbal praise when he responds to you correctly. As the puppy learns to do what you want him to do, the food rewards are gradually eliminated and only the praise remains. If you were to keep up with the food treats, you could have two problems on your hands—an obese dog and a beggar.

Training begins the minute your Leonberger puppy steps through the doorway of your home, so don't make the mistake of putting the puppy on the floor and telling him by your actions to "Go for it! Run wild!" You must act as if you know what you're doing: be the boss. An uncertain pup may be terrified to move, while a bold one will be ready to take you at your word and start plotting to destroy the house! Before you collected your puppy, you decided where his own special place would be, and that's

OUR CANINE KIDS

"Everything I learned about parenting, I learned from my dog." How often adults recognize that their parenting skills are mere extensions of the education they acquired while caring for their dogs. Many owners refer to their dogs as their "kids" and treat their canine companions like real members of the family. Surveys indicate that a majority of dog owners talk to their dogs regularly, celebrate their dogs' birthdays and purchase Christmas gifts for their dogs. Another survey shows that dog owners take their dogs to the veterinarian more frequently than they visit their own physicians.

where to put him when you first arrive home. Give him a house tour after he has investigated his area and had a nap and a bathroom "pit stop."

It's worth mentioning here that, if you've adopted an adult dog that is completely trained to your liking, lucky you! You're off the hook! However, if that dog spent his life up to this point in a kennel, or even in a good home but without any real training, be prepared to tackle the job ahead. A dog three years of age or older with no previous training cannot be blamed for not knowing what he was never taught. While the dog is trying to understand and learn your rules, at the same time he has to unlearn many of his previously self-taught habits and general view of the world.

Working with a professional

It may seem as if the last thing on a puppy's mind is the lesson at hand, when there's exploring to be done. It is up to you, as the trainer, to keep training interesting and the pup's attention focused.

SMILE WHEN YOU ORDER ME AROUND!
While trainers recommend practicing with your dog every day, it's perfectly acceptable to take a "mental health day" off. It's better not to train the dog on days when you're in a sour mood. Your bad attitude or lack of interest will be sensed by your dog, and he will respond accordingly. Studies show that dogs are well tuned in to their humans' emotions. Be conscious of how you use your voice when talking to your dog. Raising your voice or shouting will only erode your dog's trust in you as his trainer and master.

trainer will speed up your progress with an adopted adult dog. You'll need patience, too. Some new rules may be close to impossible for the dog to accept. After all, he's been successful so far by doing everything his way! (Patience again.) He may agree with your instruction for a few days and then slip back into his old ways, so you must be just as consistent and understanding in your teaching as you would be with a puppy. (More patience needed yet again!) Your dog has to learn to pay attention to your voice, your family, the daily routine, new smells, new sounds and, in some cases, even a new climate.

One of the most important things to find out about a newly adopted adult dog is his reaction to children (yours and others), strangers and your friends, and how he acts upon meeting other dogs. If he was not socialized with dogs as a puppy, this could be a major problem. This does not mean that he's a "bad" dog, a vicious dog or an aggressive dog; rather, it means that he has no idea how to read another dog's body language. There's no way for him to tell whether the other dog is a friend or foe. Survival instinct

takes over, telling him to attack first and ask questions later. This definitely calls for professional help and, even then, may not be a behavior that can be corrected 100% reliably (or even at all). If you have a puppy, this is why it is so very important to introduce your young puppy properly to other puppies and "dog-friendly" adult dogs.

A well-trained and well-socialized Leo should behave politely when meeting new people.

HOUSE-TRAINING YOUR LEONBERGER

Dogs are "touch-sensitive" when it comes to house-training. In other words, they respond to the surface on which they are given approval to eliminate. The choice is yours (the dog's version is in parentheses): The lawn (including the neighbors' lawns)? A bare patch of earth under a tree (where people like to sit and relax in the

---

TIME TO PLAY!

Playtime can happen both indoors and out. A young puppy is growing so rapidly that he needs sleep more than he needs a lot of physical exercise. Puppies get sufficient exercise on their own just through normal puppy activity. Monitor play with young children so you can remove the puppy when he's had enough, or calm the kids if they get too rowdy. Almost all puppies love to chase after a toy you've thrown, and you can turn your games into educational activities. Every time your puppy brings the toy back to you, say "Give it" (or "Drop it") followed by "Good dog" and throwing it again. If he's reluctant to give it to you, offer a small treat so that he drops the toy as he takes the treat. He will soon get the idea.

TIPS FOR
TRAINING AND SAFETY

1. Whether on or off leash, practice only in a fenced area.
2. Remove the training collar when the training session is over.
3. Don't try to break up a dog-fight.
4. "Come," "Leave it" and "Wait" are safety commands.
5. The dog belongs in a crate or behind a barrier when riding in the car.
6. Don't ignore the dog's first sign of aggression. Aggression only gets worse, so take it seriously.
7. Keep the faces of children and dogs separated.
8. Pay attention to what the dog is chewing.
9. Keep the vet's number near your phone.
10. "Okay" is a useful release command.

Breeders commonly use some type of paper to line their whelping pens, so young puppies learn to associate paper with relieving themselves. Do not use paper to line your pup's crate, as this will signal to your puppy that it is OK to urinate in his crate.

summertime)? Concrete steps or patio (all sidewalks, garages and basement floors)? The curbside (watch out for cars)? A small area of crushed stone in a corner of the yard (mine!)? The latter is the best choice if you can manage it, because it will remain strictly for the dog's use and is easy to keep clean.

You can start out with paper-training indoors and switch over to an outdoor surface as the puppy matures and gains control over his need to eliminate. For the nay-sayers, don't worry—this won't mean that the dog will soil on every piece of newspaper lying

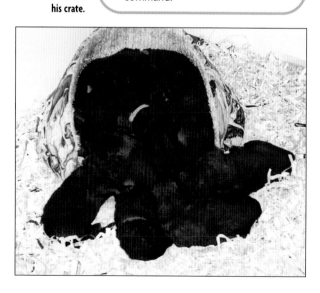

around the house. You are training him to go outside, remember? Starting out by paper-training often is the only choice for a city dog.

WHEN YOUR PUPPY'S "GOT TO GO"
Your puppy's need to relieve himself is seemingly non-stop, but signs of improvement will be seen each week. From 8 to 10 weeks old, the puppy will have to be taken outside every time he wakes up, about 10–15 minutes after every meal and after every period of play—all day long, from first thing in the morning until his bedtime! That's a total of ten or

more trips per day to teach the puppy where it's okay to relieve himself. With that schedule in mind, you can see that house-training a young puppy is not a part-time job. It requires someone to be home all day.

If that seems overwhelming or impossible, do a little planning. For example, plan to pick up your puppy at the start of a vacation period. If you can't get home in the middle of the day, plan to hire a dog-sitter or ask a neighbor to come over to take the pup outside, feed him his lunch and then take him out again about ten or so minutes after he's eaten. Also make arrangements with that or another person to be your "emergency" contact if you have

A fenced yard is ideal for house-training, as you want the puppy eventually to go to his relief area on his own.

If training one dog is a challenge, imagine dealing with a whole pack! Here is Mathias Schroeder in Germany with some of his brood of 17 Leos.

Canine Development Schedule

It is important to understand how and at what age a puppy develops into adulthood. If you are a puppy owner, consult the following Canine Development Schedule to determine the stage of development your puppy is currently experiencing. This knowledge will help you as you work with the puppy in the weeks and months ahead.

Period	Age	Characteristics
First to Third	**Birth to Seven Weeks**	Puppy needs food, sleep and warmth and responds to simple and gentle touching. Needs mother for security and disciplining. Needs littermates for learning and interacting with other dogs. Pup learns to function within a pack and learns pack order of dominance. Begin socializing pup with adults and children for short periods. Pup begins to become aware of his environment.
Fourth	**Eight to Twelve Weeks**	Brain is fully developed. Pup needs socializing with outside world. Remove from mother and littermates. Needs to change from canine pack to human pack. Human dominance necessary. Fear period occurs between 8 and 12 weeks. Avoid fright and pain.
Fifth	**Thirteen to Sixteen Weeks**	Training and formal obedience should begin. Less association with other dogs, more with people, places, situations. Period will pass easily if you remember this is pup's change-to-adolescence time. Be firm and fair. Flight instinct prominent. Permissiveness and over-disciplining can do permanent damage. Praise for good behavior.
Juvenile	**Four to Eight Months**	Another fear period about 7 to 8 months of age. It passes quickly, but be cautious of fright and pain. Sexual maturity reached. Dominant traits established. Dog should understand sit, down, come and stay by now.

Note: These are approximate time frames. Allow for individual differences in puppies.

to stay late on the job. Remind yourself—repeatedly—that this hectic schedule improves as the puppy gets older.

HOME WITHIN A HOME

Your Leonberger puppy needs to be confined to one secure, puppy-proof area when no one is able to watch his every move. Generally the kitchen is the place of choice because the floor is washable. Likewise, it's a busy family area that will accustom the pup to a variety of noises, everything from pots and pans to the telephone, blender and dishwasher. He will also be enchanted by the smell of your cooking (and will never be

Still in the whelping pen, Stormchaser Max cuddles up in his corner with a furry pal.

critical when you burn something). An exercise pen (also called an "ex-pen," a puppy version of a playpen) within the room of choice is an excellent means of confinement for a young pup. He can see out and has a certain amount of space in which to run about, but he is safe from dangerous things like electrical cords, heating units, trash baskets or open kitchen-supply cabinets. Place the pen where the puppy will not get a blast of heat or air conditioning.

In the pen, you can put a few toys, his bed (which can be his crate if the dimensions of pen and crate are compatible) and a few layers of newspaper in one small corner, just in case. A water bowl can be hung at a convenient height on the side of the ex-pen to avoid his splashing water all over the place—as Leos will do! His food dish can go on the floor.

POTTY COMMAND

Most dogs love to please their masters; there are no bounds to what dogs will do to make their owners happy. The potty command is a good example of this theory. If toileting on command makes the master happy, then more power to him. Puppies will obligingly piddle if it really makes their keepers smile. Some owners can be creative about which word they will use to command their dogs to relieve themselves. Some popular choices are "Potty," "Tinkle," "Piddle," "Let's go," "Hurry up" and "Toilet." Give the command every time your puppy goes into position and the puppy will begin to associate his business with the command.

Crates are something that pet owners are at last getting used to for their dogs. Wild or domestic canines have always preferred to sleep in den-like safe spots, and that is exactly what the crate provides. How often have you seen adult dogs that choose to sleep under a table or chair even though they have full run of the house? It's the den connection.

In your "happy" voice, use the word "Crate" every time you put the pup into his den. If he's new to a crate, toss in a small biscuit for him to chase the first few times. At night, after he's been outside, he should sleep in his crate. The crate may be kept in his designated area at night or, if you want to be sure to hear those wake-up yips in the morning, put the crate in a corner of your bedroom. However, don't make any response whatsoever to whining or crying. If he's

Keeping an eye on how much water your Leo pup is drinking, and when, will help you to anticipate when he will need to "go."

completely ignored, he'll settle down and get to sleep.

Good bedding for a young puppy is an old folded bath towel or an old blanket, something that is easily washable and disposable if necessary ("accidents" will happen!). Never put newspaper in the puppy's crate. Also, those old ideas about adding a clock to replace his mother's heartbeat, or a hot-water bottle to replace her warmth, are just that—old ideas. The clock could drive the puppy

nuts, and the hot-water bottle could end up as a very soggy waterbed! An extremely good breeder would have introduced your puppy to the crate by letting two pups sleep together for a couple of nights, followed by several nights alone. How thankful you will be if you found that breeder!

Safe toys in the pup's crate or area will keep him occupied, but monitor their condition closely. Discard any toys that show signs of being chewed to bits. Squeaky parts, bits of stuffing or plastic or any other small pieces can cause intestinal blockage or possibly choking if swallowed.

PROGRESSING WITH POTTY-TRAINING

After you've taken your puppy out and he has relieved himself in the area you've selected, he can have some free time with the family as long as there is someone responsible for watching him. That doesn't mean just someone in the same room who is watching TV or busy on the computer, but one person who is doing nothing other than keeping an eye on the pup, playing with him on the floor and helping him understand his position in the pack.

This first taste of freedom will let you begin to set the house rules. If you don't want the dog on the furniture, now is the time to prevent his first attempts to jump up onto the couch. The word to use in this case is "Off," not "Down." "Down" is the word you will use to teach the down position, which is something entirely different.

Most corrections at this stage come in the form of simply distracting the puppy. Instead of telling him "No" for "Don't chew the carpet," distract the chomping puppy with a toy and he'll

SOMEBODY TO BLAME

House-training a puppy can be frustrating for the puppy and the owner alike. The puppy does not instinctively understand the difference between defecating on the pavement outside and on the ceramic tile in the kitchen. He is confused and frightened by his human's exuberant reactions to his natural urges. The owner, arguably the more intelligent of the duo, is also frustrated that he cannot convince his puppy to obey his commands and instructions.

In frustration, the owner may struggle with the temptation to discipline the puppy, scold him or even strike him on the rear end. Not only is this type of correction unacceptable and unnecessary, it also will defeat your purpose in gaining your puppy's trust and respect. Don't blame your nine-week-old puppy. Blame yourself for not being 100% consistent in the puppy's lessons and routine. The lesson here is simple: try harder and your puppy will succeed.

DAILY SCHEDULE

How many relief trips does your puppy need per day? A puppy up to the age of 14 weeks will need to go outside about 8 to 12 times per day! You will have to take the pup out any time he starts sniffing around the floor or turning in small circles, as well as after naps, meals, games and lessons or whenever he's released from his crate. Once the puppy is 14 to 22 weeks of age, he will require only 6 to 8 relief trips. At the ages of 22 to 32 weeks, the puppy will require about 5 to 7 trips. Adult dogs typically require 4 relief trips per day, in the morning, afternoon, evening and late at night.

the puppy outside to relieve himself. If you are paper-training, put him back into his confined area on the newspapers. In either case, praise him as he eliminates while he actually is in the act of relieving himself. Three seconds after he has finished is too late! You'll be praising him for running toward you, or picking up a toy or whatever he may be doing at that moment, and that's not what you want to be praising him for. Timing is a vital tool in all dog training. Use it.

Remove soiled newspapers immediately and replace them with clean ones. You may want to take a small piece of soiled paper and place it in the middle of the new clean papers, as the scent will attract him to that spot when it's time to go again. That scent attraction is why it's so important to clean up any messes made in the house by using a product specially made to eliminate the odor of dog urine and droppings. Regular household cleansers won't do the trick. Pet shops sell the best pet deodorizers. Invest in the largest container you can find.

Scent attraction eventually will lead your pup to his chosen spot outdoors; this is the basis of outdoor training. When you take your puppy outside to relieve himself, use a one-word command such as "Outside" or "Go-potty" (that's one word to the puppy!) as you pick him up and attach his

hopefully forget about the carpet.

As you are playing with the pup, do not forget to watch him closely and pay attention to his body language. Whenever you see him begin to circle or sniff, take leash. Then put him down in his area. If for any reason you can't carry him, snap the leash on quickly and lead him to his spot. Now comes the hard part—hard for you, that is. Just stand there until he urinates and defecates. Move him a few feet in one direction or another if he's just sitting there looking at you, but remember that this is neither playtime nor time for a walk. This is strictly a business trip! Then, as he circles and squats (remember your timing!), give him a quiet "Good dog" as praise. If you start to jump for joy, ecstatic over his performance, he'll do one of two things: either he will stop mid-stream, as it were, or he'll do it again for you—in the house—and expect you to be just as delighted!

Give him five minutes or so and, if he doesn't go in that time, take him back indoors to his confined area and try again in another ten minutes, or immediately if you see him sniffing and circling. By careful observation, you'll soon work out a successful schedule.

CREATURES OF HABIT

Canine behaviorists and trainers aptly describe dogs as "creatures of habit," meaning that dogs respond to structure in their daily lives and welcome a routine. Do not interpret this to mean that dogs enjoy endless repetition in their training sessions. Dogs get bored just as humans do. Keep training sessions interesting and exciting. Vary the commands and the locations in which you practice. Give short breaks for play in between lessons. A bored student will never be the best performer in the class.

Accidents, by the way, are just that—accidents. Clean them up quickly and thoroughly, without comment, after the puppy has been taken outside to finish his business and then put back into his area or crate. If you witness an accident in progress, say "No!" in a stern voice and get the pup outdoors immediately. No punishment is needed. You and your puppy are just learning each other's language, and sometimes it's easy to miss a puppy's message. Chalk it up to experience and watch more closely from now on.

KEEPING THE PACK ORDERLY

Discipline is a form of training that brings order to life. For example, military discipline is what allows the soldiers in an

Once he's trained to his potty location, going there on his own to do his business will be just another part of the daily routine.

BE UPSTANDING!
You are the dog's leader. During training, stand up straight so your dog looks up at you, and therefore up *to* you. Say the command words distinctly, in a clear, declarative tone of voice. (No barking!) Give rewards only as the correct response takes place (remember your timing!). Praise, smiles and treats are "rewards" used to positively reinforce correct responses. Don't repeat a mistake. Just change to another exercise—you will soon find success!

army to work as one. Discipline is a form of teaching and, in dogs, is the basis of how the successful pack operates. Each member knows his place in the pack and all respect the leader, or Alpha dog. It is essential for your puppy that you establish this type of relationship, with you as the Alpha, or leader. It is a form of social coexistence that all canines recognize and accept. Discipline, therefore, is never to be confused with punishment. When you teach your puppy how you want him to behave, and he behaves

properly and you praise him for it, you are disciplining him with a form of positive reinforcement.

For a dog, rewards come in the form of praise, a smile, a cheerful tone of voice, a few friendly pats or a rub of the ears. Rewards are also small food treats. Obviously, that does not mean bits of regular dog food. Instead, treats are very small bits of special things like cheese or pieces of soft dog treats. The idea is to reward the dog with something very small that he can taste and swallow, providing instant positive reinforcement. If he has to take time to chew the treat, by the time he is finished he will have forgotten what he did to earn it!

Your puppy should never be physically punished. The displeasure shown on your face and in your voice is sufficient to signal to the pup that he has done something wrong. He wants to please everyone higher up on the social ladder, especially his leader, so a scowl and harsh voice will take care of the error. Growling out the word "Shame!" when the pup is caught in the act of doing something wrong is better than the repetitive "No." Some dogs hear "No" so often that they begin to think it's their name! By the way, do not use the dog's name when you're correcting him. His name is reserved to get his attention for something pleasant about to take place.

There are punishments that have nothing to do with you. For example, your dog may think that chasing cats is one reason for his existence. You can try to stop it as much as you like but without success, because it's such fun for the dog. But one good hissing, spitting, swipe of a cat's claws across the dog's nose will put an end to the game forever. Intervene only when your dog's eyeball is seriously at risk. Cat scratches can cause permanent damage to an innocent but annoying puppy.

PUPPY KINDERGARTEN

COLLAR AND LEASH

Before you begin your Leonberger puppy's education, he must be used to his collar and leash. Choose a collar for your puppy that is secure, but not heavy or bulky. He won't enjoy training if he's uncomfortable. A flat buckle collar is fine for everyday wear and for initial puppy training. For older dogs, there are several types of training collars such as the martingale, which is a double loop that tightens slightly around the neck, and the head collar, which is similar to a horse's halter or the "half-check," which also tightens slightly. The martingale is usually made of nylon and the half-check of leather, both of which will not damage the coat around the Leo's neck. Do not use a chain choke

DON'T STRESS ME OUT
Your dog doesn't have to deal with paying the bills, the daily commute, PTA meetings and the like, but, believe it or not, there's a lot of stress in a dog's world. Stress can be caused by the owner's impatient demeanor and his angry or harsh corrections. If your dog cringes when you reach for his training collar, he's stressed. An older dog is sometimes stressed out when he goes to a new home. No matter what the cause, put off all training until he's over it. If he's going through a fear period—shying away from people, trembling when spoken to, avoiding eye contact or hiding under furniture—wait to resume training. Naturally you'd also postpone your lessons if the dog were sick, and the same goes for you. Show some compassion.

Dogs respond better to petting and praise than to punishment—let your Leo know that he's done well.

collar with your Leo. You may not be disposed to use a chain choke collar even if your breeder has told you that it's suitable for your Leonberger.

A lightweight 6-foot woven cotton or nylon training leash is preferred by most trainers because it is easy to fold up in your hand and comfortable to hold because there is a certain amount of give to it. There are lessons where the dog will start off 6 feet away from you at the end of the leash. The leash used to take the puppy outside to relieve himself is shorter because you don't want him to roam away from his area. The shorter leash will also be the one to use when you walk the puppy.

If you've been wise enough to enroll in a Puppy Kindergarten training class, suggestions will be made as to the best collar and leash for your young puppy. I say "wise" because your puppy will be in a class with puppies in his age range (up to five months old) of all breeds and sizes. It's the perfect way for him to learn the right way (and the wrong way) to interact with other dogs as well as their people. You cannot teach your puppy how to interpret another dog's sign language. For a first-time puppy owner, these socialization classes are invaluable. For experienced dog owners, they are a real boon to further training.

ATTENTION

You've been using the dog's name since the minute you collected him from the breeder, so you should be able to get his attention by saying his name—with a big smile and in an excited tone of voice. His response will be the puppy equivalent of "Here I am! What are we going to do?" Your immediate response (if you haven't guessed by now) is "Good dog." Rewarding him at the moment he pays attention to you teaches him the proper way to respond when he hears his name.

EXERCISES FOR A BASIC CANINE EDUCATION

THE SIT EXERCISE

There are several ways to teach the puppy to sit. The first one is

BASIC PRINCIPLES OF DOG TRAINING

1. Start training early. A young puppy is ready, willing and able.
2. Timing is your all-important tool. Praise at the exact time that the dog responds correctly. Pay close attention.
3. Patience is almost as important as timing!
4. Repeat! The same word has to mean the same thing every time.
5. In the beginning, praise all correct behavior verbally, along with treats and petting.

A SIMPLE "SIT"

When you command your dog to sit, use the word "Sit." Do not say "Sit down," as your dog will not know whether you mean "Sit" or "Down," or maybe you mean both. Be clear in your instructions to your dog; use one-word commands and always be consistent.

to catch him whenever he is about to sit and, as his backside nears the floor, say "Sit, good dog!" That's positive reinforcement and, if your timing is sharp, he will learn that what he's doing at that second is connected to your saying "Sit" and that you think he's clever for doing it!

Another method is to start with the puppy on his leash in front of you. Show him a treat in the palm of your right hand. Bring your hand up under his nose and, almost in slow motion, move your hand up and back so his nose goes up in the air and his head tilts back as he follows the treat in your hand. At that point, he will have to either sit or fall over, so as his back legs buckle under, say "Sit, good dog," and then give him the treat and lots of praise. You may have to begin with your hand lightly running up his chest, actually lifting his chin up until he sits. Some (usually older) dogs require gentle pressure on their hindquarters with the left hand, in which case the dog should be on your left side. Puppies generally do not appreciate this physical dominance.

After a few times, you should be able to show the dog a treat in the open palm of your hand, raise your hand waist-high as you say "Sit" and have him sit. Once again, you have taught him two things at the same time. Both the verbal command and the motion of the hand are signals for the sit. Your puppy is watching you almost more than he is listening to you, so what you do is just as important as what you say.

Don't save any of these drills only for training sessions. Use them as much as possible at odd times during a normal day. The dog should always sit before being given his food dish. He should sit

Sit is a basic command and is the foundation of many other exercises; for example, the heel exercise begins and ends with the dog sitting at the trainer's left side.

DOWN

"Down" is a harsh-sounding word and a submissive posture in dog body language, thus presenting two obstacles in teaching the down command. When the dog is about to flop down on his own, tell him "Good down." Pups that are not good about being handled learn better by having food lowered in front of them. A dog that trusts you can be gently guided into position. When you give the command "Down," be sure to say it sweetly!

it may not be fun, the reward of your approval is worth his effort.

Start with the puppy on your left side in a sit position. Hold the leash right above his collar in your left hand. Have an extra-special treat, such as a small piece of cooked chicken or hot dog, in your right hand. Place it at the end of the pup's nose and steadily move your hand down and forward along the ground. Hold the leash to prevent a sudden lunge for the food. As the puppy goes into the down position, say "Down" very gently.

The difficulty with this exercise is twofold: it's both the submissive aspect and the fact that most people say the word "Down" as if they were a drill sergeant in charge of recruits! So issue the command sweetly, give him the treat and have the pup maintain the down position for several seconds. If he tries to get up immediately, place your hands on his shoulders and press down gently, giving him a very quiet "Good dog." As you progress with this lesson, increase the "down time" until he will hold it until you say "Okay" (his cue for release). Practice this one in the house at various times throughout the day.

By increasing the length of time during which the dog must maintain the down position, you'll find many uses for it. For example, he can lie at your feet in

to let you go through a doorway first, when the doorbell rings or when you stop to speak to someone on the street.

THE DOWN EXERCISE

Before beginning to teach the down command, you must consider how the dog feels about this exercise. To him, "down" is a submissive position. Being flat on the floor with you standing over him is not his idea of fun. It's up to you to let him know that, while the vet's office or anywhere that both of you have to wait, when you are on the phone, while the family is eating and so forth. If you progress to training for competitive obedience, he'll already be all set for the exercise called the "long down."

THE STAY EXERCISE

You can teach your Leonberger to stay in the sit, down and stand positions. To teach the sit/stay, have the dog sit on your left side. Hold the leash at waist level in your left hand and let the dog know that you have a treat in your closed right hand. Step forward on your right foot as you say "Stay." Immediately turn and stand directly in front of the dog, keeping your right hand up high so he'll keep his eye on the treat hand and maintain the sit

In the sit/stay, the trainer's hand signal, along with vocal command, tells the dog to stay until he is given the "Okay."

position for a count of five. Return to your original position and offer the reward.

Increase the length of the sit/stay each time until the dog can hold it for at least 30 seconds without moving. After about a week of success, move out on your right foot and take two steps before turning to face the dog. Give the "Stay" hand signal (left palm back toward the dog's head) as you leave. He gets the treat when you return and he holds the sit/stay. Increase the distance that you walk away from him before turning until you reach the length of your training leash. But don't rush it! Go back to the beginning if he moves before he should. No matter what the lesson, never be upset by having to back up for a few days. The repetition and practice are what will make your dog reliable in these commands. It won't do any good to move on to something more difficult if the command is not mastered at the

READY, SIT, GO!

On your marks, get set: train! Most professional trainers agree that the sit command is the place to start your dog's formal education. Sitting is a natural posture for most dogs, and they respond to the sit exercise willingly and readily. For every lesson, begin with the sit command so that you start out on a successful note; likewise, you should practice the sit command at the end of every lesson as well, because you always want to end on a high note.

The trainer's outstretched arms act as a release signal, telling the dog to come to the trainer.

THE COME EXERCISE

No command is more important to the safety of your Leonberger than "Come." It is what you should say every single time you see the puppy running toward you: "Binky, come! Good dog." During playtime, run a few feet away from the puppy and turn and tell him to "Come" as he is already running to you. You can go so far as to teach your puppy two things at once if you squat down and hold out your arms. As the pup gets close to you and you're

easier levels. Above all, even if you do get frustrated, never let your puppy know! Always keep a positive, upbeat attitude during training, which will transmit to your dog for positive results.

The down/stay is taught in the same way once the dog is completely reliable and steady with the down command. Again, don't rush it. With the dog in the down position on your left side, step out on your right foot as you say "Stay." Return by walking around in back of the dog and into your original position. While you are training, it's okay to murmur something like "Hold on" to encourage him to stay put. When the dog will stay without moving when you are at a distance of 3 or 4 feet, begin to increase the length of time before you return. Be sure he holds the down on your return until you say "Okay." At that point, he gets his treat—just so he'll remember for next time that it's not over until it's over.

COME AND GET IT!

The come command is your dog's safety signal. Until he is 99% perfect in responding, don't use the come command if you cannot enforce it. Practice on leash with treats or squeakers, or whenever the dog is running to you. Never call him to come to you if he is to be corrected for a misdemeanor. Reward the dog with a treat and happy praise whenever he comes to you.

OKAY!

This is the signal that tells your dog that he can quit whatever he was doing. Use "Okay" to end a session on a correct response to a command. (Never end on an incorrect response.) Lots of praise follows. People use "Okay" a lot and it has other uses for dogs, too. Your dog is barking. You say, "Okay! Come!" "Okay" signals him to stop the barking activity and "Come" allows him to come to you for a "Good dog."

saying "Good dog," bring your right arm in about waist high. Now he's also learning the hand signal, an excellent device should you be on the phone when you need to get him to come to you! You'll also both be one step ahead when you enter obedience classes.

When the puppy responds to your well-timed "Come," try it with the puppy on the training leash. This time, catch him off guard, while he's sniffing a leaf or watching a bird: "Binky, come!" You may have to pause for a split second after his name to be sure you have his attention. If the puppy shows any sign of confusion, give the leash a mild jerk and take a couple of steps backward. Do not repeat the command. In this case, you should say "Good come" as he reaches you.

That's the number-one rule of

training. Each command word is given just once. Anything more is nagging. You'll also notice that all commands are one word only. Even when they are actually two words, you say them as one.

Never call the dog to come to you—with or without his name— if you are angry or intend to correct him for some misbehavior. When correcting the pup, you go to him. Your dog must always connect "Come" with something pleasant and with your approval; then you can rely on his response.

Puppies, like children, have notoriously short attention spans, so don't overdo it with any of the training. Keep each lesson short. Break it up with a quick run around the yard or a ball toss, repeat the lesson and quit as soon as the pup gets it right. That way, you will always end with a "Good dog."

Life isn't perfect and neither are puppies. A time will come, often around ten months of age, when he'll become "selectively deaf" or choose to "forget" his name. He may respond by wagging his tail (and even seeming to smile at you) with a look that says "Make me!" Laugh, throw his favorite toy and skip the lesson you had planned. Pups will be pups!

THE HEEL EXERCISE

The second most important command to teach, after the come,

Your eight-to ten-week-old puppy will probably follow you everywhere, but that's his natural instinct, not your control over the situation. However, any time he does follow you, you can say "Heel" and be ahead of the game, as he will learn to associate this command with the action of following you before you even begin teaching him to heel.

There is a very precise, almost military, procedure for teaching your dog to heel. As with all other obedience training, begin with the dog on your left side. He will be in a very nice sit and you will have the training leash across your chest. Hold the loop and folded leash in your right hand. Pick up the slack leash above the dog in your left hand and hold it loosely at your side. Step out on your left foot as you say "Heel." If the puppy does not move, give a gentle tug or pat your left leg to

While all dogs, pet or show, should be trained to heel, show dogs must heel properly in the ring as the judge evaluates their movement. is the heel. When you are walking your growing puppy, you need to be in control. Besides, it looks terrible to be pulled and yanked down the street, and it's not much fun either. If you think being pulled by a puppy is difficult, imagine what walking an untrained adult Leonberger would be like!

Encountering people and other dogs on your walks is inevitable. How your Leo will react depends largely on the training and socialization you provide.

back into position and begin again. With a really determined puller, try switching to a head collar. This will automatically turn the pup's head toward you so you can bring him back easily to the heel position. Give quiet, reassuring praise every time the leash goes slack and he's staying with you.

get him started. If he surges ahead of you, stop and pull him back gently until he is at your side. Tell him to sit and begin again.

Walk a few steps and stop while the puppy is correctly beside you. Tell him to sit and give mild verbal praise. (More enthusiastic praise will encourage him to think the lesson is over.) Repeat the lesson, increasing the number of steps you take only as long as the dog is heeling nicely beside you. When you end the lesson, have him hold the sit, then give him the "Okay" to let him know that this is the end of the lesson. Praise him so that he knows he did a good job.

The cure for excessive pulling (a common problem) is to stop when the dog is no more than 2 or 3 feet ahead of you. Guide him

Taking your Leo for walks should be part of his daily exercise, so heel training is a must.

LET'S GO!

Many people use "Let's go" instead of "Heel" when teaching their dogs to behave on lead. It sounds more like fun! When beginning to teach the heel, whatever command you use, always step off on your left foot. That's the one next to the dog, who is on your left side, in case you've forgotten. Keep a loose leash. When the dog pulls ahead, stop, bring him back and begin again. Use treats to guide him around turns.

Boden with an
obedience
dumbbell.
Retrieving the
dumbbell is an
advanced
obedience
exercise.

Staying and heeling can take a lot out of a dog, so provide playtime and free-running exercise to shake off the stress when the lessons are over. You don't want him to associate training with all work and no fun.

TAPERING OFF TIDBITS
Your dog has been watching you—and the hand that treats—throughout all of his lessons, and now it's time to break the treat habit. Begin by giving him treats at the end of each lesson only. Then start to give a treat after the end of only some of the lessons. At the end of every lesson, as well as during the lessons, be consistent with the praise. Your pup now doesn't know whether he'll get a treat or not, but he should keep performing well just in case! Finally, you will stop giving treat rewards entirely. Save them for something brand-new that you want to teach him. Keep up the praise and you'll always have a "good dog."

OBEDIENCE CLASSES
The advantages of an obedience class are that your dog will have to learn amid the distractions of other people and dogs and that your mistakes will be quickly corrected by the trainer. Teaching your dog along with a qualified instructor and other handlers who may have more dog experience

Swimming,
retrieving and
working in water
are among the
multi-talented
Leonberger's
skills.

than you is another plus of the class environment. The instructor and other handlers can help you to find the most efficient way of teaching your dog a command or exercise. It's often easier to learn by other people's mistakes than your own. You will also learn all of the requirements for competitive obedience trials, in which you can earn titles and go on to advanced jumping and retrieving exercises, which are fun for many dogs. Obedience classes build the foundation needed for many other canine activities (in which we humans are allowed to participate, too!).

OTHER ACTIVITIES

Whether a dog is trained in the structured environment of a class or alone with his owner at home, there are many activities that can bring fun and rewards to both owner and dog once they have mastered basic control.

Carting, or draft work, is still the special passion of the Leonberger, so it is no surprise that this activity is extremely popular with the dog as well as its like-minded owner. The Leonberger excels in carting and possesses natural ability for this sport. Carting is also popular with owners of Bernese Mountain Dogs and other mountain dogs.

In both Switzerland and Sweden, draft-dog trials are conducted, with special courses designed specifically for this purpose. The dogs' appetite for draft work is so strong that owners have difficulty controlling their dogs' impatience and enthusiasm during the harnessing and at the starting line. The harnesses and carts are a major part of the carting spectacle, with beautiful handwork on the harnesses and elaborate decorations on the carts.

Breed and kennel clubs in other countries also host working trials to enable the carting breeds to utilize their talents in a productive, and often competitive, venue. As a leisure activity, just for fun, many dogs of various drafting breeds in Switzerland and Germany have been shown in working harness at parades, club events and other public outings.

Teaching the dog to help out around the home, in the yard or on the farm provides great

FLYBALL FAME
Leonbergers have begun to leave their mark on flyball competitions. In America, the first Leonberger has attained the FD (Flyball Dog) title and, in the UK, a Leo named Ersteen earned the FD and FDI (Flyball Dog Intermediate).

satisfaction to both dog and owner. In addition, the dog's help makes life a little easier for his owner and raises his stature as a valued companion to his family. It helps give the dog a purpose by occupying his mind and providing an outlet for his energy.

Backpacking is an exciting and healthy activity that the fully-grown dog can be taught without assistance from more than his owner. The exercise of walking and climbing is good for man and dog alike, and the bond that they develop together is priceless. The rule for backpacking with any dog is never to expect the dog to carry more than one-sixth of his body weight.

If you are interested in participating in organized competition with your Leonberger, there are activities other than obedience shows and drafting trials in which you and your dog can become involved. Agility is a popular sport where dogs run through an obstacle course that includes various jumps, tunnels and other

WHO'S TRAINING WHOM?

Dog training is a black-and-white exercise. The correct response to a command must be absolute, and the trainer must insist on completely accurate responses from the dog. A trainer cannot command his dog to sit and then settle for the dog's melting into the down position. Often owners are so pleased that their dogs "did something" in response to a command that they just shrug and say, "OK, Down" even though they wanted the dog to sit. You want your dog to respond to the command without hesitation: he must respond at that moment and correctly every time.

exercises to test the dog's speed and coordination. While there are not too many Leonbergers seen in agility competition, those that do compete can fare well. Despite their large size, Leonbergers are quite agile dogs. On the agility course, the owners run beside their dogs to give commands and to guide them through the course. Although competitive, the focus is on fun—it's fun to do, fun to watch and great exercise.

As a Leonberger owner, you also have the opportunity to participate in water trials with your dog. These are often sponsored by Newfoundland clubs with an open invitation to their cousin, the Leonberger.

A Leonberger club's members taking their dogs for a walk. Joining a breed club is a wonderful way to meet and become friends with people who share your love for the Leo.

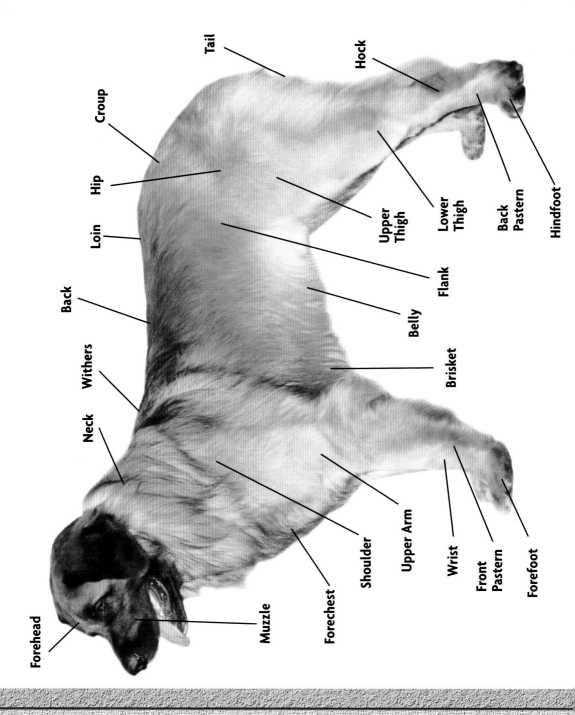

Tail

Hock

Croup

Hip

Back Pastern

Hindfoot

Loin

Upper Thigh

Lower Thigh

Back

Flank

Withers

Belly

Neck

Brisket

Forehead

Muzzle

Forechest

Shoulder

Upper Arm

Wrist

Front Pastern

Forefoot

PHYSICAL STRUCTURE OF THE LEONBERGER

LEONBERGER

By Lowell Ackerman DVM, DACVD

HEALTHCARE FOR A LIFETIME
When you own a dog, you become his healthcare advocate over his entire lifespan, as well as being the one to shoulder the financial burden of such care. Accordingly, it is worthwhile to focus on prevention rather than treatment, as you and your pet will both be happier.

Of course, the best place to have begun your program of preventive healthcare is with the initial purchase or adoption of your dog. There is no way of guaranteeing that your new furry friend is free of medical problems, but there are some things you can do to improve your odds. You certainly should have done adequate research into the Leo and have selected your puppy carefully rather than buying on impulse. Health issues aside, a large number of pet abandonment and relinquishment cases arise from a mismatch between pet needs and owner expectations. This is entirely preventable with appropriate planning and finding a good breeder.

Regarding healthcare issues specifically, it is very difficult to make blanket statements about where to acquire a problem-free pet, but, again, a reputable breeder is your best bet. In an ideal situation, you have the opportunity to see both parents, get references from other owners of the breeder's pups and see genetic-testing

TAKING YOUR DOG'S TEMPERATURE

It is important to know how to take your dog's temperature at times when you think he may be ill. It's not the most enjoyable task, but it can be done without too much difficulty. It's easier with a helper, preferably someone with whom the dog is friendly, so that one of you can hold the dog while the other inserts the thermometer.

Before inserting the thermometer, coat the end with petroleum jelly. Insert the thermometer slowly and gently into the dog's rectum about one inch. Wait for the reading, about two minutes. Be sure to remove the thermometer carefully and clean it thoroughly after each use.

A dog's normal body temperature is between 100.5 and 102.5 degrees F. Immediate veterinary attention is required if the dog's temperature is below 99 or above 104 degrees F.

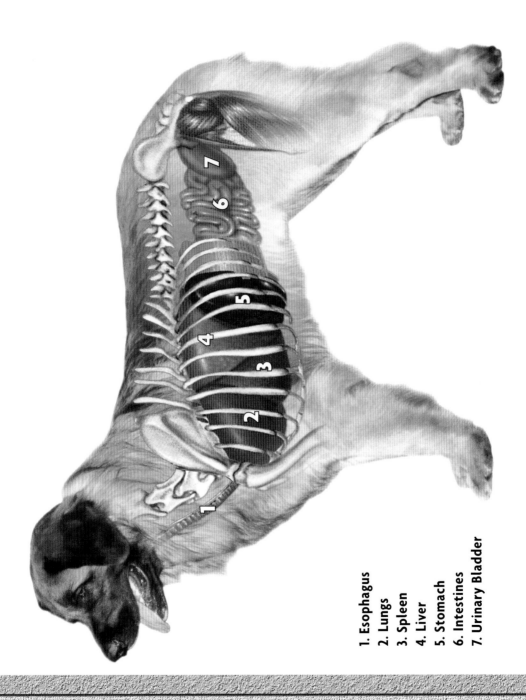

1. Esophagus
2. Lungs
3. Spleen
4. Liver
5. Stomach
6. Intestines
7. Urinary Bladder

INTERNAL ORGANS OF THE LEONBERGER

documentation for several generations of the litter's ancestors. At the very least, you must thoroughly investigate the Leonberger and the problems inherent in that breed, as well as the genetic testing available to screen for those problems. Genetic testing offers some important benefits, but testing is

available for only a few disorders in a relatively small number of breeds and is not available for some of the most common genetic diseases, such as hip dysplasia, cataracts, epilepsy, cardiomyopathy, etc. This area of research is indeed exciting and increasingly important, and advances will continue to be made each year. In fact, recent research has shown that there is an equivalent dog gene for 75% of known human genes, so research done in either species is likely to benefit the other.

We've also discussed that evaluating the behavioral nature of your Leo and that of his immediate family members is an important part of the selection process that cannot be underestimated or underemphasized. It is sometimes difficult to evaluate temperament in puppies because certain behavioral tendencies, such as some forms of aggression, may not be immediately evident. More dogs are euthanized each year for behavioral reasons than for all medical conditions combined, so it is critical to take temperament issues seriously. Start with a well-balanced, friendly companion and put the time and effort into proper socialization, and you will both be rewarded with a lifelong valued relationship.

Assuming that you have started off with a pup from healthy, sound stock, you then become responsible for helping your veterinarian keep

PROBLEM: AND THAT STARTS WITH "P"

Urinary tract problems more commonly affect female dogs, especially those who have been spayed. The first sign that a urinary tract problem exists usually is a strong odor from the urine or an unusual color. Blood in the urine, known as hematuria, is another sign of an infection, related to cystitis, a bladder infection, bladder cancer or a blood-clotting disorder. Urinary tract problems can also be signaled by the dog's straining while urinating, experiencing pain during urination and genital discharge as well as excessive water intake and urination.

Excessive drinking, in and of itself, does not indicate a urinary tract problem. A dog who is drinking more than normal may have a kidney or liver problem, a hormonal disorder or diabetes mellitus. Behaviorists report a disorder known as psychogenic polydipsia, which manifests itself in excessive drinking and urination. If you notice your dog drinking much more than normal, take him to the vet.

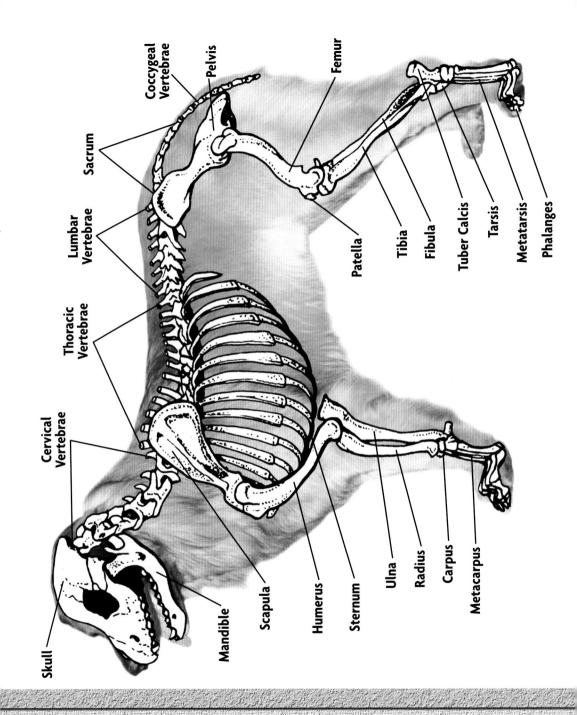

Coccygeal Vertebrae

Pelvis

Femur

Sacrum

Tuber Calcis

Tarsis

Metatarsis

Phalanges

Patella

Tibia

Fibula

Lumbar Vertebrae

Thoracic Vertebrae

Cervical Vertebrae

Mandible

Scapula

Humerus

Sternum

Ulna

Radius

Carpus

Metacarpus

Skull

SKELETAL STRUCTURE OF THE LEONBERGER

your pet healthy. Some crucial things happen before you even bring your puppy home. Parasite control typically begins at two weeks of age, and vaccinations typically begin at six to eight weeks of age. A pre-pubertal evaluation is typically scheduled for about six months of age. At this time, a dental evaluation is done (since the adult teeth are now in), heartworm prevention is started and neutering or spaying is most commonly done.

It is critical to commence regular dental care at home if you have not already done so. It may not sound very important, but most dogs have active periodontal disease by four years of age if they don't have their teeth cleaned regularly at home, not just at their veterinary exams. Dental problems lead to more than just bad "doggy breath." Gum disease can have very serious medical consequences. If you start brushing your dog's teeth and using antiseptic rinses from a young age, your dog will be accustomed to it and will not resist. The results will be healthy dentition, which your pet will need to enjoy a long, healthy life.

Most dogs are considered adults at a year of age, although the Leo still has some filling out to do after his first birthday. Even individual dogs within each breed have different healthcare requirements, so work with your veterinarian to determine what will be needed and what your role should

> ### DOGGIE DENTAL DON'TS
> A veterinary dental exam is necessary if you notice one or any combination of the following in your dog:
> - Broken, loose or missing teeth
> - Loss of appetite (which could be due to mouth pain or illness caused by infection)
> - Gum abnormalities, including redness, swelling and bleeding
> - Drooling, with or without blood
> - Yellowing of the teeth or gumline, indicating tartar
> - Bad breath

be. This doctor-client relationship is important, because as vaccination guidelines change, there may not be an annual "vaccine visit" scheduled. You must make sure that you see your veterinarian at least annually, even if no vaccines are due, because this is the best opportunity to coordinate healthcare activities and to make sure that no medical issues creep by unaddressed.

When your Leo reaches three-quarters of his anticipated lifespan, he is considered a "senior" and likely requires some special care. The Leo's average lifespan is 10–11 years, with some living into their teens; thus, the Leo will be a senior at about seven years old. In general, if you've been taking great care of your canine companion throughout his formative and adult years, the transition to senior status should be

Number-One Killer Disease in Dogs: CANCER

In every age, there is a word associated with a disease or plague that causes humans to shudder. In the 21st century, that word is "cancer." Just as cancer is the leading cause of death in humans, it claims nearly half the lives of dogs that die from a natural disease as well as half the dogs that die over the age of ten years.

Described as a genetic disease, cancer becomes a greater risk as the dog ages. Vets and dog owners have become increasingly aware of the threat of cancer to dogs. Statistics reveal that one dog in every five will develop cancer, the most common of which is skin cancer. Many cancers, including prostate, ovarian and breast cancer, can be avoided by spaying and neutering our dogs by the age of six months. Cancer is the disease responsible for the most deaths in the Leonberger, with bone cancer and hemangiosarcoma (cancer of certain blood-vessels linings) being the most common type seen in the breed.

Early detection of cancer can save or extend a dog's life, so it is absolutely vital for owners to have their dogs examined by a qualified vet or oncologist immediately upon detection of any abnormality. Certain dietary guidelines have also proven to reduce the onset and spread of cancer. Foods based on fish rather than beef, due to the presence of Omega-3 fatty acids, are recommended. Other amino acids such as glutamine have significant benefits for canines, particularly those breeds that show a greater susceptibility to cancer.

Cancer management and treatments promise hope for future generations of canines. Since the disease is genetic, breeders should never breed a dog whose parents, grandparents and any related siblings have developed cancer. It is difficult to know whether to exclude an otherwise healthy dog from a breeding program, as the disease does not manifest itself until the dog's senior years.

RECOGNIZE CANCER WARNING SIGNS

Since early detection can possibly rescue your dog from becoming a cancer statistic, it is essential for owners to recognize the possible signs and seek the assistance of a qualified professional.

- Abnormal bumps or lumps that continue to grow
- Bleeding or discharge from any body cavity
- Persistent stiffness or lameness
- Recurrent sores or sores that do not heal
- Inappetence
- Breathing difficulties
- Weight loss
- Bad breath or odors
- General malaise and fatigue
- Eating and swallowing problems
- Difficulty urinating and defecating

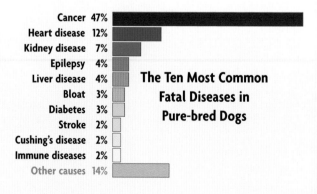

Cancer	47%
Heart disease	12%
Kidney disease	7%
Epilepsy	4%
Liver disease	4%
Bloat	3%
Diabetes	3%
Stroke	2%
Cushing's disease	2%
Immune diseases	2%
Other causes	14%

The Ten Most Common Fatal Diseases in Pure-bred Dogs

a smooth one. Age is not a disease, and as long as everything is functioning as it should, there is no reason why most of late adulthood should not be rewarding for both you and your pet. This is especially true if you have tended to the details, such as regular veterinary visits, proper dental care, excellent nutrition and management of bone and joint issues.

At this stage in your Leo's life, your veterinarian may want to schedule visits twice yearly, instead of once, to run some laboratory screenings, electrocardiograms and the like, and to change the diet to something more digestible. Catching problems early is the best way to manage them effectively. Treating the early stages of heart disease is so much easier than trying to intervene when there is more significant damage to the heart muscle. Similarly, managing the beginning of kidney problems is fairly routine if there is no significant kidney damage. Other problems, like cognitive dysfunction (similar to senility and Alzheimer's disease), cancer, diabetes and arthritis, are more common in older dogs, but all can be treated to help the dog live as many happy, comfortable years as possible. Just as in people, medical management is more effective (and less expensive) when you catch things early.

SELECTING A VETERINARIAN

There is probably no more important decision that you will make regarding your pet's healthcare than the selection of his doctor. Your pet's veterinarian will be a pediatrician, family-practice physician and gerontologist, depending on the dog's life stage, and will be the individual who makes recommendations regarding issues such as when specialists need to be consulted, when diagnostic testing and/or therapeutic intervention is needed and when you will need to seek outside emergency and critical-care services. Your vet will act as your advocate and liaison throughout these processes.

Everyone has his own idea about what to look for in a vet, an individual who will play a big role in his dog's (and, of course, his own) life for many years to come. For some, it is the compassionate caregiver with whom they hope to develop a professional relationship to span the lives of their dogs and even their future pets. For others, they are seeking a clinician with keen diagnostic and therapeutic insight who can deliver state-of-the-art healthcare. Still others need a veterinary facility that is open evenings and weekends, or is in close proximity or provides mobile veterinary services, to accommodate their schedules; these people may not much mind that their dogs might see different veterinarians on

Do You Know about Hip Dysplasia?

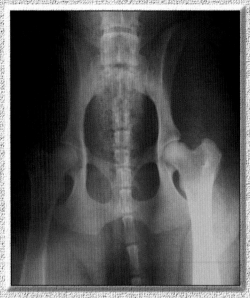

X-ray of a dog with "Good" hips.

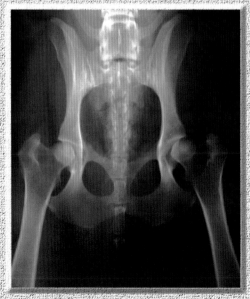

X-ray of a dog with "Moderate" dysplastic hips.

Hip dysplasia is a fairly common condition found in pure-bred dogs. When a dog has hip dysplasia, his hind leg has an incorrectly formed hip joint. By constant use of the hip joint, it becomes more and more loose, wears abnormally and may become arthritic.

Hip dysplasia can only be confirmed with an x-ray, but certain symptoms may indicate a problem. Your dog may have a hip dysplasia problem if he walks in a peculiar manner, hops instead of smoothly runs, uses his hind legs in unison (to keep the pressure off the weak joint), has trouble getting up from a prone position or always sits with both legs together on one side of his body.

As the dog matures, he may adapt well to life with a bad hip, but in a few years the arthritis develops and many dogs with hip dysplasia become crippled.

Hip dysplasia is considered an inherited disease and can be diagnosed definitively by x-ray only when the dog is two years old, although symptoms often appear earlier. Some experts claim that a special diet might help your puppy outgrow the bad hip, but the usual treatments are surgical. The removal of the pectineus muscle, the removal of the round part of the femur, reconstructing the pelvis and replacing the hip with an artificial one are all surgical interventions that are expensive, but they are usually very successful. Follow the advice of your veterinarian.

each visit. Just as we have different reasons for selecting our own healthcare professionals (e.g., covered by insurance plan, expert in field, convenient location, etc.), we should not expect that there is a one-size-fits-all recommendation for selecting a veterinarian and veterinary practice. The best advice is to be honest in your assessment of what you expect from a veterinary practice and to conscientiously research the options in your area. You will quickly appreciate that not all veterinary practices are the same, and you will be happiest with one that truly meets your needs.

There is another point to be considered in the selection of veterinary services. Not that long ago, a single veterinarian would attempt to manage all medical and surgical issues as they arose. That was often problematic, because veterinarians are trained in many breeds, species and diseases, and it was just impossible for general veterinary practitioners to be experts in every animal, every field and every ailment. However, just as in the human healthcare fields, specialization has allowed general practitioners to concentrate on primary healthcare delivery, especially wellness and the prevention of infectious diseases, and to utilize a network of specialists to assist in the management of conditions that require specific expertise and experience. Thus

YOUR DOG NEEDS TO VISIT THE VET IF:

- He has ingested a toxin such as antifreeze or a toxic plant; in these cases, administer first aid and call the vet right away
- His teeth are discolored, loose or missing or he has sores or other signs of infection or abnormality in the mouth
- He has been vomiting, has had diarrhea or has been constipated for over 24 hours; call immediately if you notice blood
- He has refused food for over 24 hours
- His eating habits, water intake or toilet habits have noticeably changed; if you have noticed weight gain or weight loss
- He shows symptoms of bloat, which requires *immediate* attention
- He is salivating excessively
- He has a lump in his throat
- He has a lumps or bumps anywhere on the body
- He is very lethargic
- He appears to be in pain or otherwise has trouble chewing or swallowing
- His skin loses elasticity

Of course, there will be other instances in which a visit to the vet is necessary; these are just some of the signs that could be indicative of serious problems that need to be caught as early as possible.

Veteran bitch Rossnick Joie de Vivre, still looking great!

Veteran bitch Rossnick Joie de Vivre, still looking great!

there are now many types of veterinary specialists, including dermatologists, cardiologists, ophthalmologists, surgeons, internists, oncologists, neurologists, behaviorists, criticalists and others to help primary-care veterinarians deal with complicated medical challenges. In most cases, specialists see cases referred by primary-care veterinarians, make diagnoses and set up management plans. From there, the animals' ongoing care is returned to their primary-care veterinarians. This important team approach to your pet's medical-care needs has provided opportunities for advanced care and an unparalleled level of quality to be delivered.

With all of the opportunities for your Leo to receive high-quality veterinary medical care, there is another topic that needs to be addressed at the same time—cost. It's been said that you can have excellent healthcare or inexpensive healthcare, but never both; this is as true in veterinary medicine as it is in human medicine. While veterinary costs are a fraction of what the same services cost in the human healthcare arena, it is still difficult to deal with unanticipated medical costs, especially since they can easily creep into hundreds or even thousands of dollars if specialists or emergency services become involved. However, there are ways of managing these risks. The easiest is to buy pet health insurance and realize that its foremost purpose is not to cover routine healthcare visits but rather to serve as an umbrella for those rainy days when your pet needs medical care and you don't want to worry about whether or not you can afford that care.

Pet insurance policies are very cost-effective (and very inexpensive by human health-insurance standards), but make sure that you buy the policy long before you intend to use it (preferably starting in puppyhood, because coverage will exclude pre-existing conditions) and that you are actually buying an indemnity insurance plan from an insurance company that is regulated by your state or province. Many insurance policy look-alikes are actually discount clubs that are redeemable only at specific locations and for specific services. An indemnity plan covers your pet at almost all veterinary, specialty and emergency practices and is an excellent way to manage your pet's ongoing health-care needs.

VACCINATIONS AND INFECTIOUS DISEASES

There has never been an easier time to prevent a variety of infectious diseases in your dog, but the advances we've made in veterinary medicine come with a price—choice. Now while it may seem that choice is a good thing (and it is), it has never been more difficult for the pet owner (or the veterinarian) to make an informed decision about the best way to protect pets through vaccination.

Years ago, it was just accepted that puppies got a starter series of vaccinations and then annual

"boosters" throughout their lives to keep them protected. As more and more vaccines became available, consumers wanted the convenience of having all of that protection in a single injection. The result was "multivalent" vaccines that crammed a lot of protection into a single syringe. The manufacturers' recommendations were to give the vaccines annually, and this was a simple enough protocol to follow. However, as veterinary medicine has become more sophisticated and we have started looking more at healthcare quandaries rather than convenience, it became necessary to reevaluate the situation and deal with some tough questions. It is important to realize that whether or not to use a particular vaccine depends on the risk of contracting the disease against which it protects, the severity of the disease if it is contracted, the duration of

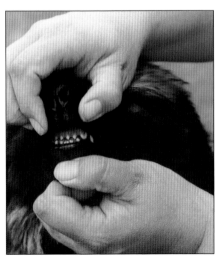

Owners should monitor the Leo puppy's teeth to ensure that the permanent teeth emerge properly.

COMMON INFECTIOUS DISEASES

Let's discuss some of the diseases that create the need for vaccination in the first place. Following are the major canine infectious diseases and a simple explanation of each.

Rabies: A devastating viral disease that can be fatal in dogs and people. In fact, vaccination of dogs and cats is an important public-health measure to create a resistant animal buffer population to protect people from contracting the disease. Vaccination schedules are determined on a government level and are not optional for pet owners; rabies vaccination is required by law in all 50 states.

Parvovirus: A severe, potentially life-threatening disease that is easily transmitted between dogs. There are four strains of the virus, but it is believed that there is significant "cross-protection" between strains that may be included in individual vaccines.

Distemper: A potentially severe and life-threatening disease with a relatively high risk of exposure, especially in certain regions. In very high-risk distemper environments, young pups may be vaccinated with human measles vaccine, a related virus that offers cross-protection when administered at four to ten weeks of age.

Hepatitis: Caused by canine adenovirus type 1 (CAV-1), but since vaccination with the causative virus has a higher rate of adverse effects, cross-protection is derived from the use of adenovirus type 2 (CAV-2), a cause of respiratory disease and one of the potential causes of canine cough. Vaccination with CAV-2 provides long-term immunity against hepatitis, but relatively less protection against respiratory infection.

Canine cough: Also called tracheobronchitis, actually a fairly complicated result of viral and bacterial offenders; therefore, even with vaccination, protection is incomplete. Wherever dogs congregate, canine cough will likely be spread among them. Intranasal vaccination with *Bordetella* and parainfluenza is the best safeguard, but the duration of immunity does not appear to be very long, typically a year at most. These are non-core vaccines, but vaccination is sometimes mandated by boarding kennels, obedience classes, dog shows and other places where dogs congregate to try to minimize spread of infection.

Leptospirosis: A potentially fatal disease that is more common in some geographic regions. It is capable of being spread to humans. The disease varies with the individual "serovar," or strain, of *Leptospira* involved. Since there does not appear to be much cross-protection between serovars, protection is only as good as the likelihood that the serovar in the vaccine is the same as the one in the pet's local environment. Problems with *Leptospira* vaccines are that protection does not last very long, side effects are not uncommon and a large percentage of dogs (perhaps 30%) may not respond to vaccination.

Borrelia burgdorferi: The cause of Lyme disease, the risk of which varies with the geographic area in which the pet lives and travels. Lyme disease is spread by deer ticks in the eastern US and western black-legged ticks in the western part of the country, and the risk of exposure is high in some regions. Lameness, fever and inappetence are most commonly seen in affected dogs. The extent of protection from the vaccine has not been conclusively demonstrated.

Coronavirus: This disease has a high risk of exposure, especially in areas where dogs congregate, but it typically causes only mild to moderate digestive upset (diarrhea, vomiting, etc.). Vaccines are available, but the duration of protection is believed to be relatively short and the effectiveness of the vaccine in preventing infection is considered low.

There are many other vaccinations available, including those for *Giardia* and canine adenovirus-1. While there may be some specific indications for their use, and local risk factors to be considered, they are not widely recommended for most dogs.

immunity provided by the vaccine, the safety of the product and the needs of the individual animal. In a very general sense, rabies, distemper, hepatitis and parvovirus are considered core vaccine needs, while parainfluenza, *Bordetella bronchiseptica*, leptospirosis, coronavirus and borreliosis (Lyme disease) are considered non-core needs and best reserved for animals that demonstrate reasonable risk of contracting the diseases.

NEUTERING/SPAYING
Sterilization procedures (neutering for males/spaying for females) are meant to accomplish several purposes. While the underlying premise is to address the risk of pet overpopulation, there are also some medical and behavioral benefits to the surgeries as well. For females, spaying prior to the first estrus (heat cycle) leads to a marked reduction in the risk of mammary cancer. There also will be no manifestations of "heat" to attract male dogs and no bleeding in the house. For males, there is prevention of testicular cancer and a reduction in the risk of prostate problems. In both sexes, there may be some limited reduction in aggressive behaviors toward other dogs, and some diminishing of urine marking, roaming and mounting.

While neutering and spaying do indeed prevent animals from

SAMPLE VACCINATION SCHEDULE

6–8 weeks of age	Parvovirus, Distemper, Adenovirus-2 (Hepatitis)
9–11 weeks of age	Parvovirus, Distemper, Adenovirus-2 (Hepatitis)
12–14 weeks of age	Parvovirus, Distemper, Adenovirus-2 (Hepatitis)
16–20 weeks of age	Rabies
1 year of age	Parvovirus, Distemper, Adenovirus-2 (Hepatitis), Rabies

Revaccination is performed every one to three years, depending on the product, the method of administration and the patient's risk. Initial adult inoculation (for dogs at least 16 weeks of age in which a puppy series was not done or could not be confirmed) is two vaccinations, done three to four weeks apart, with revaccination according to the same criteria mentioned. Other vaccines are given as decided between owner and veterinarian.

contributing to pet overpopulation, even no-cost and low-cost neutering options have not eliminated the problem. Perhaps one of the main reasons for this is that individuals that intentionally breed their dogs and those that allow their animals to run at large are the main causes of unwanted offspring. Also, animals in shelters are often there because they were abandoned or relinquished, not because they came from unplanned matings. Neutering/spaying is important, but it should be considered in the context of the real causes of animals' ending up in shelters and eventually being euthanized.

One of the important considerations regarding neutering is that it is a surgical procedure. This sometimes gets lost in discussions of low-cost procedures and commoditization of the process. In females, spaying is specifically referred to as an ovariohysterectomy. In this procedure, a midline incision is made in the abdomen and the entire uterus and both ovaries are surgically removed. While this is a major invasive surgical procedure, it usually has few complications, because it is typically performed on healthy young animals. However, it is major surgery, as any woman who has had a hysterectomy will attest.

In males, neutering has traditionally referred to castration, which involves the surgical removal of both testicles. While still a significant piece of surgery, there is not the abdominal exposure that is required in the female surgery. In addition, there is now a chemical sterilization option, in which a solution is injected into each testicle, leading to atrophy of the sperm-producing cells. This can typically be done under sedation rather than full anesthesia. This is a relatively new approach, and there are no long-term clinical studies yet available.

Neutering/spaying is typically done around six months of age at most veterinary hospitals, although techniques have been pioneered to perform the procedures in animals as young as eight weeks of age. In general, the surgeries on the very young animals are done for the specific reason of sterilizing them before they go to their new homes. This is done in some shelter hospitals for assurance that the animals will definitely not produce any pups. Otherwise, these organizations need to rely on owners to comply with their wishes to have the animals "altered" at a later date, something that does not always happen.

There are some exciting immunocontraceptive "vaccines" currently under development, and there may be a time when contraception in pets will not require surgical procedures. We anxiously await these developments.

Guarding the Leo's Health

The LCA's Health, Research and Education Committee states on its website, www.leowatch.org, that its "mission is to identify, research, and educate the public about health issues facing the Leonberger." Working in close partnership with this committee is the Leonberger Health Foundation (www.leohealth.org).

As the Leonberger population grows, so does the number of health problems seen in the breed. Thus, these committees are working hard to identify problems and their mode of inheritance so that breeders can breed hereditary problems out of their lines and eventually out of the breed as a whole through careful selection of healthy breeding animals. In the meantime, knowing as much as possible about dogs' health backgrounds is the best way to keep these diseases under control. The health committees rely on Leo owners to report problems in their dogs in order to document their occurrences and direct their research.

Following are brief explanations of some of the Leonberger's main health conditions not previously mentioned:

- *Addison's disease:* A condition in which adrenal gland function is low, thus negatively affecting areas such as metabolism, stress response and blood pressure. Research is focused on finding genetic markers.
- *Allergies:* Skin and ear problems can result from allergies to food or similar sensitivities; food allergies often are successfully treated through diet management.
- *Elbow dysplasia:* Lameness caused by various disorders affecting the elbow joint. It is detected by x-ray and can be managed therapeutically or surgically in more severe cases. As with hip dysplasia, dogs' elbows should be graded by the OFA.
- *Eye problems:* Eye disorders seen in the breed include cataracts, ectropion and entropion, progressive retinal atrophy, persistent pupillary membrane, lens luxation and glaucoma. Eye testing with the Canine Eye Registration Foundation (CERF) is recommended annually up to five years of age, and then every other year. CERF registers dogs for breeding purposes.
- *Heart disease:* Dilated cardiomyopathy is the main heart problem seen in the breed, usually, but not always, in older dogs.
- *Hypothyroidism:* A hereditary form of this condition is seen in the Leonberger. It can be diagnosed through a blood test and is relatively easy to treat with medication.
- *Inherited polyneuropathy:* This refers to serious neurological disorders affecting the nerves that stimulate muscles; it is also called LP/PN (laryngeal paralysis and polyneuropathy). LP affects the larynx, causing a dog to wheeze, have trouble breathing, barking, eating and drinking. PN usually manifests itself in the legs, leading to lack of coordination. Research is being done to determine genetic markers and develop successful treatments.
- *Kidney/liver problems:* Although only seen in a small number of dogs, these are significant because it is fatal in those affected.
- *Missing teeth:* A long-time concern in the breed, more prevalent in certain lines. The breed standard states that a Leo must have full dentition.
- *Osteochondrosis dissecans (OCD):* Abnormal development of cartilage in certain joints that causes pain and worsens with age; arthritis eventually can result. It occurs as a combination of genetic predisposition and environmental factors.

For more detailed information on these and all health concerns in the Leonberger, please visit the LCA's health website and that of the Leonberger Health Foundation.

A scanning electron micrograph of a dog flea, *Ctenocephalides canis*, on dog hair.

EXTERNAL PARASITES

FLEAS

Fleas have been around for millions of years and, while we have better tools now for controlling them than at any time in the past, there still is little chance that they will end up on an endangered species list. Actually, they are very well adapted to living on our pets, and they continue to adapt as we make advances.

The female flea can consume 15 times her weight in blood during active reproduction and can lay as many as 40 eggs a day. These eggs are very resistant to the effects of insecticides. They hatch into larvae, which then mature and spin cocoons. The immature fleas reside in this pupal stage until the time is right for feeding. This pupal stage is also very resistant to the effects of insecticides, and pupae can last in the environment without feeding for many months. Newly emergent fleas are attracted to animals by the warmth of the animals' bodies, movement and exhaled carbon dioxide. However, when they first emerge from their cocoons, they orient towards light; thus when an animal passes between a flea and the light source, casting a shadow, the flea pounces and starts to feed. If the animal turns out to be a dog or cat, the reproductive cycle continues. If the flea lands on another type of animal, including a person, the flea will bite but will then look for a more appropriate host. An emerging adult flea can survive without feeding for up to 12 months but, once it tastes blood, it can survive off its host for only three to four days.

It was once thought that fleas spend most of their lives in the environment, but we now know that fleas won't willingly jump off a dog unless leaping to another dog or when physically removed by brushing, bathing or other manipulation. Flea eggs, on the other hand, are shiny and smooth, and they roll off the animal and into the environment. The eggs, larvae and pupae then exist in the environment, but once the adult finds a susceptible animal, it's home sweet home until the flea is forced to seek refuge elsewhere.

Since adult fleas live on the animal and immature forms survive in the environment, a successful treatment plan must address all stages of the flea life cycle. There are now several safe and effective flea-control products that can be applied on a monthly

> ### FLEA PREVENTION FOR YOUR DOG
> - Discuss with your veterinarian the safest product to protect your dog, likely in the form of a monthly tablet or a liquid preparation placed on the back of the dog's neck.
> - For dogs suffering from flea-bite dermatitis, a shampoo or topical insecticide treatment is required.
> - Your lawn and property should be sprayed with an insecticide designed to kill fleas and ticks that lurk outdoors.
> - Using a flea comb, check the dog's coat regularly for any signs of parasites.
> - Practice good housekeeping. Vacuum floors, carpets and furniture regularly, especially in the areas that the dog frequents, and wash the dog's bedding weekly.
> - Follow up house-cleaning with carpet shampoos and sprays to rid the house of fleas at all stages of development. Insect growth regulators are the safest option.

basis. These include fipronil, imidacloprid, selamectin and permethrin (found in several formulations). Most of these products have significant flea-killing rates within 24 hours. However, none of them will control the immature forms in the environment. To accomplish this, there are a variety of insect growth regulators that can be sprayed into

THE FLEA'S LIFE CYCLE

What came first, the flea or the egg? This age-old mystery is more difficult to comprehend than the

actual cycle of the flea. Fleas usually live only about four months. A female can lay 2,000 eggs in her lifetime.

Egg

After ten days of rolling around your carpet or under your furniture, the eggs hatch into larvae,

Larva

which feed on various and sundry debris. In days or

months, depending on the climate, the larvae spin cocoons and develop into the pupal or nymph stage, which quickly develop into fleas.

Pupa

These immature fleas must locate a host within 10 to 14 days or they will die. Only about 1% of the flea population exist as adult fleas, while the other 99% exist as eggs, larvae or pupae.

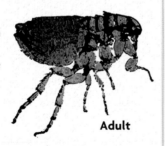

Adult

PHOTO BY CAROLINA BIOLOGICAL SUPPLY CO.

the environment (e.g., pyriprox-yfen, methoprene, fenoxycarb) as well as insect development inhibitors such as lufenuron that can be administered. These compounds have no effect on adult fleas, but they stop immature forms from developing into adults. In years gone by, we relied heavily on toxic insecti-cides (such as organophosphates, organochlorines and carbamates) to manage the flea problem, but today's options are not only much safer to use on our pets but also safer for the environment.

TICKS

Ticks are members of the spider class (arachnids) and are blood-sucking parasites capable of transmitting a variety of diseases, including Lyme disease, ehrlichiosis, babesiosis and Rocky Mountain spotted fever. It's easy to see ticks on your own skin, but it is more of a challenge when your furry companion is affected. Whenever you happen to be planning a stroll in a tick-infested area (especially forests, grassy or wooded areas or parks) be prepared to do a thorough inspection of your dog afterward to search for ticks. Ticks can be tricky, so make sure you spend time looking in the ears, between the toes and everywhere else where a tick might hide. Ticks need to be attached for 24–72 hours before they transmit most of the diseases that they carry, so you do have a window of opportunity for some preventive intervention.

Female ticks live to eat and

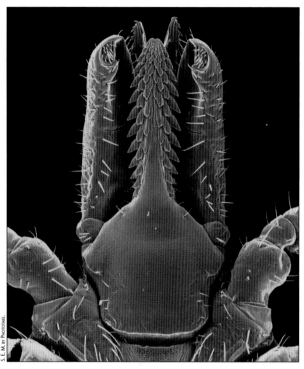

S. E. M. BY PHOTOTAKE.

A scanning electron micrograph of the head of a female deer tick, *Ixodes dammini*, a parasitic tick that carries Lyme disease.

breed. They can lay between 4,000 and 5,000 eggs and they die soon after. Males, on the other hand, live only to mate with the females and continue the process as long as they are able. Most ticks live on multiple hosts before parasitizing dogs. The immature forms typically reside on grass and shrubs, waiting for susceptible animals to walk by. The larvae and nymph stages typically feed on wildlife.

If only a few ticks are present on a dog, they can be plucked out, but it is important to remove the entire head and mouthparts, which may be deeply embedded

A TICKING BOMB

There is nothing good about a tick's harpooning his nose into your dog's skin. Among the diseases caused by ticks are Rocky Mountain spotted fever, canine ehrlichiosis, canine babesiosis, canine hepatozoonosis and Lyme disease. If a dog is allergic to the saliva of a female wood tick, he can develop tick paralysis.

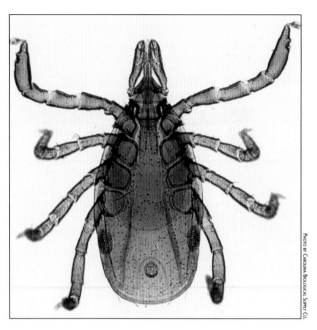

Photo by Carolina Biological Supply Co.

Deer tick,
Ixodes dammini.

in the skin. This is best accomplished with forceps designed especially for this purpose; fingers can be used but should be protected with rubber gloves, plastic wrap or at least a paper towel. The tick should be grasped as closely as possible to the animal's skin and should be pulled upward with steady, even pressure. Do not squeeze, crush or puncture the body of the tick or you risk exposure to any disease carried by that tick. Once the ticks have been removed, the sites of attachment should be disinfected. Your hands should then be washed with soap and water to further minimize risk of contagion. The tick should be disposed of in a container of

alcohol or household bleach.

Some of the newer flea products, specifically those with fipronil, selamectin and permethrin, have effect against some, but not all, species of tick. Flea collars containing appropriate pesticides (e.g., propoxur, chlorfenvinphos) can aid in tick control. In most areas, such collars should be placed on animals in March, at the beginning of the tick season, and changed regularly. Leaving the collar on when the pesticide level is waning invites the development of resistance. Amitraz collars are also good for tick control, and the active ingredient does not interfere with other flea-control products. The ingredient helps prevent the attachment of ticks to the skin and will cause those ticks already on the skin to detach themselves.

TICK CONTROL

Removal of underbrush and leaf litter and the thinning of trees in areas where tick control is desired are recommended. These actions remove the cover and food sources for small animals that serve as hosts for ticks. With continued mowing of grasses in these areas, the probability of ticks' surviving is further reduced. A variety of insecticide ingredients (e.g., resmethrin, carbaryl, permethrin, chlorpyrifos, dioxathion and allethrin) are registered for tick control around the home.

MITES

Mites are tiny arachnid parasites that parasitize the skin of dogs. Skin diseases caused by mites are referred to as "mange," and there are many different forms seen in dogs. These forms are very different from one another, each one warranting an individual description.

Sarcoptic mange, or scabies, is one of the itchiest conditions that affects dogs. The microscopic *Sarcoptes* mites burrow into the superficial layers of the skin and can drive dogs crazy with itchiness. They are also communicable to people, although they can't complete their reproductive cycle on people. In addition to being tiny, the mites also are often difficult to find when trying to make a diagnosis. Skin scrapings from multiple areas are examined microscopically but, even then, sometimes the mites cannot be found.

Fortunately, scabies is relatively easy to treat, and there are a variety of products that will successfully kill the mites. Since the mites can't live in the environment for very long without feeding, a complete cure is usually possible within four to eight weeks.

Cheyletiellosis is caused by a relatively large mite, which sometimes can be seen even without a microscope. Often referred to as "walking dandruff," this also causes itching, but not usually as profound as with scabies.

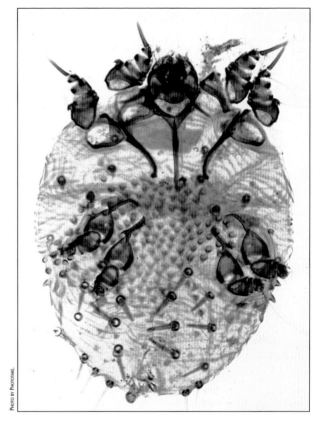

PHOTO BY PHOTOTAKE.

Sarcoptes scabiei, commonly known as the "itch mite."

While *Cheyletiella* mites can survive somewhat longer in the environment than scabies mites, they too are relatively easy to treat, being responsive to not only the medications used to treat scabies but also often to flea-control products.

Otodectes cynotis is the canine ear mite and is one of the more common causes of mange, especially in young dogs in shelters or pet stores. That's because the mites are typically present in large numbers and are quickly spread to

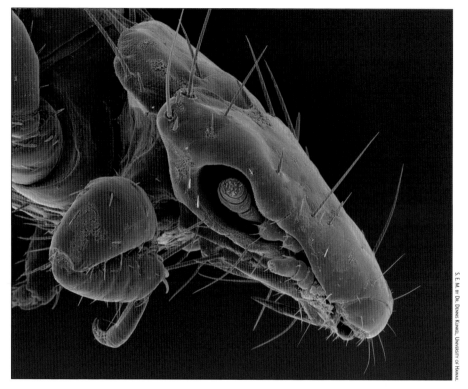

Micrograph of a dog louse, *Heterodoxus spiniger*. Female lice attach their eggs to the hairs of the dog. As the eggs hatch, the larval lice bite and feed on the blood. Lice can also feed on dead skin and hair. This feeding activity can cause hair loss and skin problems.

S. E. M. BY DR. DENNIS KUNKEL, UNIVERSITY OF HAWAII.

nearby animals. The mites rarely do much harm but can be difficult to eradicate if the treatment regimen is not comprehensive. While many try to treat the condition with ear drops only, this is the most common cause of treatment failure. Ear drops cause the mites to simply move out of the ears and as far away as possible (usually to the base of the tail) until the insecticide levels in the ears drop to an acceptable level—then it's back to business as usual! The successful treatment of ear mites requires treating all animals in the household with a systemic insecticide, such as selamectin, or a combination of miticidal ear drops combined with whole-body flea-control preparations.

Demodicosis, sometimes referred to as red mange, can be one of the most difficult forms of mange to treat. Part of the problem has to do with the fact that the mites live in the hair follicles and they are relatively well shielded from topical and systemic products. The main issue, however, is that demodectic mange typically results only when there is some underlying process interfering with the dog's immune system.

Since *Demodex* mites are

normal residents of the skin of mammals, including humans, there is usually a mite population explosion only when the immune system fails to keep the number of mites in check. In young animals, the immune deficit may be transient or may reflect an actual inherited immune problem. In older animals, demodicosis is usually seen only when there is another disease hampering the immune system, such as diabetes, cancer, thyroid problems or the use of immune-suppressing drugs. Accordingly, treatment involves not only trying to kill the mange mites but also discerning what is interfering with immune function and correcting it if possible.

Chiggers represent several different species of mite that don't parasitize dogs specifically, but do latch on to passersby and can cause irritation. The problem is most prevalent in wooded areas in the late summer and fall. Treatment is not difficult, as the mites do not complete their life cycle on dogs and are susceptible to a variety of miticidal products.

MOSQUITOES

Mosquitoes have long been known to transmit a variety of diseases to people, as well as just being biting pests during warm weather. They also pose a real risk to pets. Not only do they carry deadly heartworms but recently there also has been much concern over their involvement with West Nile virus. While we can avoid heartworm with the use of preventive medications, there are no such preventives for West Nile virus. The only method of prevention in endemic areas is active mosquito control. Fortunately, most dogs that have been exposed to the virus only developed flu-like symptoms and, to date, there have not been the large number of reported deaths in canines as seen in some other species.

Illustration of *Demodex folliculoram.*

ILLUSTRATION BY PHOTOTAKE.

MOSQUITO REPELLENT

Low concentrations of DEET (less than 10%), found in many human mosquito repellents, have been safely used in dogs but, in these concentrations, probably give only about two hours of protection. DEET may be safe in these small concentrations, but since it is not licensed for use on dogs, there is no research proving its safety for dogs. Products containing permethrin give the longest-lasting protection, perhaps two to four weeks. As DEET is not licensed for use on dogs, and both DEET and permethrin can be quite toxic to cats, appropriate care should be exercised. Other products, such as those containing oil of citronella, also have some mosquito-repellent activity, but typically have a relatively short duration of action.

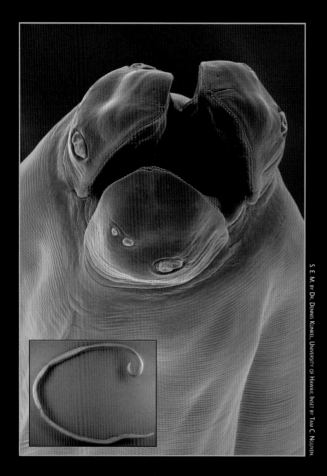

S.E.M. BY DR. DENNIS KUNKEL, UNIVERSITY OF HAWAII. INSET BY TAM C. NGUYEN.

The ascarid roundworm *Toxocara canis*, showing the mouth with three lips. INSET: Photomicrograph of the roundworm *Ascaris lumbricoides*.

INTERNAL PARASITES: WORMS

ASCARIDS

Ascarids are intestinal roundworms that rarely cause severe disease in dogs. Nonetheless, they are of major public health significance because they can be transferred to people. Sadly, it is children who are most commonly affected by the parasite, probably from inadvertently ingesting ascarid-contaminated soil. In fact, many yards and children's sandboxes contain appreciable numbers of ascarid eggs. So, while ascarids don't bite dogs or latch onto their intestines to suck blood, they do cause some nasty medical conditions in children and are best eradicated from our furry friends. Because pups can start passing ascarid eggs by three weeks of age, most parasite-control programs begin at two weeks of age and are repeated every two weeks until pups are eight weeks old. It is important to

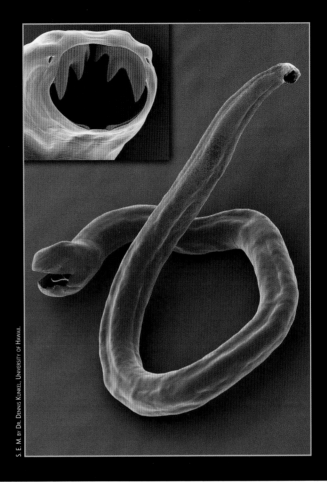

S. E. M. BY DR. DENNIS KUNKEL, UNIVERSITY OF HAWAII.

realize that bitches can pass ascarids to their pups even if they test negative prior to whelping. Accordingly, bitches are best treated at the same time as the pups.

HOOKWORMS

Unlike ascarids, hookworms do latch onto a dog's intestinal tract and can cause significant loss of blood and protein. Similar to ascarids, hookworms can be transmitted to humans, where they cause a condition known as cutaneous larval migrans. Dogs can become infected either by consuming the infective larvae or by the larvae's penetrating the skin directly. People most often get infected when they are lying on the ground (such as on a beach) and the larvae penetrate the skin. Yes, the larvae can penetrate through a beach blanket. Hookworms are typically susceptible to the same medications used to treat ascarids.

The hookworm *Ancylostoma caninum* infests the intestines of dogs. INSET: Note the row of hooks at the posterior end, used to anchor the worm to the intestinal wall.

WHIPWORMS

Whipworms latch onto the lower aspects of the dog's colon and can cause cramping and diarrhea. Eggs do not start to appear in the dog's feces until about three months after the dog was infected. This worm has a peculiar life cycle, which makes it more difficult to control than ascarids or hookworms. The good thing is that whipworms rarely are transferred to people.

Some of the medications used to treat ascarids and hookworms are also effective against whipworms, but, in general, a separate treatment protocol is needed. Since most of the medications are effective against the adults but not the eggs or larvae, treatment is typically repeated in three weeks, and then often in three

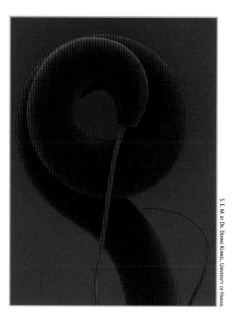

Adult whipworm, *Trichuris* sp., an intestinal parasite.

S. E. M. BY DR. DENNIS KUNKEL, UNIVERSITY OF HAWAII.

WORM-CONTROL GUIDELINES

- Practice sanitary habits with your dog and home.
- Clean up after your dog and don't let him sniff or eat other dogs' droppings.
- Control insects and fleas in the dog's environment. Fleas, lice, cockroaches, beetles, mice and rats can act as hosts for various worms.
- Prevent dogs from eating uncooked meat, raw poultry and dead animals.
- Keep dogs and children from playing in sand and soil.
- Kennel dogs on cement or gravel; avoid dirt runs.
- Administer heartworm preventives regularly.
- Have your vet examine your dog's stools at your annual visits.
- Select a boarding kennel carefully so as to avoid contamination from other dogs or an unsanitary environment.
- Prevent dogs from roaming. Obey local leash laws.

months as well. Unfortunately, since dogs don't develop resistance to whipworms, it is difficult to prevent them from getting reinfected if they visit soil contaminated with whipworm eggs.

TAPEWORMS

There are many different species of tapeworm that affect dogs, but *Dipylidium caninum* is probably the most common and is spread by fleas. Flea larvae feed on organic debris and tapeworm eggs in the environment and, when a dog chews at himself and manages to ingest fleas, he might get a dose of tapeworm at the same time. The tapeworm then develops further in the intestine of the dog.

The tapeworm itself, which is a parasitic flatworm that latches onto the intestinal wall, is composed of numerous segments. When the segments break off into the intestine (as proglottids), they may accumulate around the rectum, like grains of rice. While this tapeworm is disgusting in its behavior, it is not directly communicable to humans (although humans can also get infected by swallowing fleas).

A much more dangerous flatworm is *Echinococcus multilocularis*, which is typically found in foxes, coyotes and wolves. The eggs are passed in the feces and infect rodents, and, when dogs eat the rodents, the dogs can be infected by thousands of adult tapeworms. While the parasites don't cause many problems in dogs, this is considered the most lethal worm infection that people can get. Take appropriate precautions if you live in an area in which these tapeworms are found. Do not use mulch that may contain feces of dogs, cats or wildlife, and

discourage your pets from hunting wildlife. Treat these tapeworm infections aggressively in pets, because if humans get infected, approximately half die.

HEARTWORMS

Heartworm disease is caused by the parasite *Dirofilaria immitis* and is seen in dogs around the world. A member of the roundworm group, it is spread between dogs by the bite of an infected mosquito. The mosquito injects infective larvae into the dog's skin with its bite, and these larvae develop under the skin for a period of time before making their way to the heart. There they develop into adults, which grow and create blockages of the heart, lungs and major blood vessels there. They also start

A dog tapeworm proglottid (body segment).

The dog tapeworm *Taenia pisiformis*.

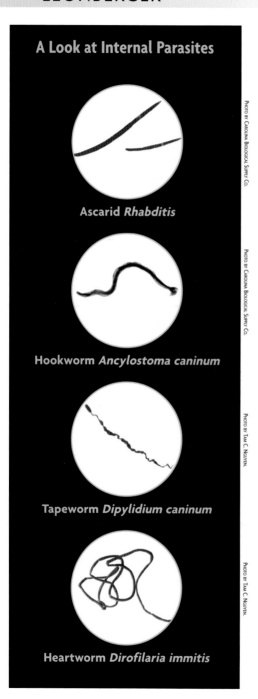

A Look at Internal Parasites

Ascarid *Rhabditis*

PHOTO BY CAROLINA BIOLOGICAL SUPPLY CO.

Hookworm *Ancylostoma caninum*

PHOTO BY CAROLINA BIOLOGICAL SUPPLY CO.

Tapeworm *Dipylidium caninum*

PHOTO BY TAM C. NGUYEN

Heartworm *Dirofilaria immitis*

PHOTO BY TAM C. NGUYEN

producing offspring (microfilariae) and these microfilariae circulate in the bloodstream, waiting to hitch a ride when the next mosquito bites. Once in the mosquito, the microfilariae develop into infective larvae and the entire process is repeated.

When dogs get infected with heartworm, over time they tend to develop symptoms associated with heart disease, such as coughing, exercise intolerance and potentially many other manifestations. Diagnosis is confirmed by either seeing the microfilariae themselves in blood samples or using immunologic tests (antigen testing) to identify the presence of adult heartworms. Since antigen tests measure the presence of adult heartworms and microfilarial tests measure offspring produced by adults, neither are positive until six to seven months after the initial infection. However, the beginning of damage can occur by fifth-stage larvae as early as three months after infection. Thus it is possible for dogs to be harboring problem-causing larvae for up to three months before either type of test would identify an infection.

The good news is that there are great protocols available for preventing heartworm in dogs. Testing is critical in the process, and it is important to understand the benefits as well as the limitations of such testing. All dogs six months of age or older that have not been on continuous heartworm-

Life Cycle of the Heartworm

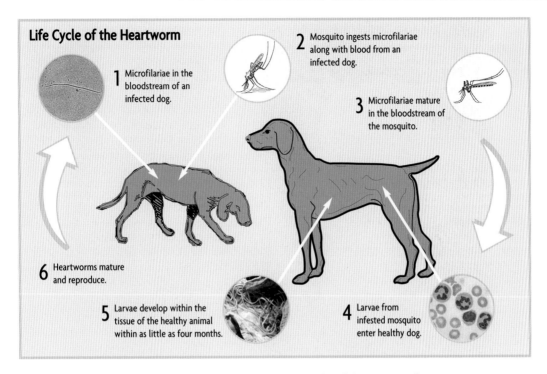

1 Microfilariae in the bloodstream of an infected dog.

2 Mosquito ingests microfilariae along with blood from an infected dog.

3 Microfilariae mature in the bloodstream of the mosquito.

4 Larvae from infested mosquito enter healthy dog.

5 Larvae develop within the tissue of the healthy animal within as little as four months.

6 Heartworms mature and reproduce.

preventive medication should be screened with microfilarial or antigen tests. For dogs receiving preventive medication, periodic antigen testing helps assess the effectiveness of the preventives. The American Heartworm Society guidelines suggest that annual retesting may not be necessary when owners have absolutely provided continuous heartworm prevention. Retesting on a two- to three-year interval may be sufficient in these cases. However, your veterinarian will likely have specific guidelines under which heartworm preventives will be prescribed, and many prefer to err on the side of safety and retest annually.

It is indeed fortunate that heartworm is relatively easy to prevent, because treatments can be as life-threatening as the disease itself. Treatment requires a two-step process that kills the adult heartworms first and then the microfilariae. Prevention is obviously preferable; this involves a once-monthly oral or topical treatment. The most common oral preventives include ivermectin (not suitable for some breeds), moxidectin and milbemycin oxime; the once-a-month topical drug selamectin provides heartworm protection in addition to flea, tick and other parasite controls.

THE **ABC**S OF
Emergency Care

Abrasions
Clean wound with running water or 3% hydrogen peroxide. Pat dry with gauze and spray with antibiotic. Do not cover.

Animal Bites
Clean area with soap and saline solution or water. Apply pressure to any bleeding area. Apply antibiotic ointment.

Antifreeze Poisoning
Induce vomiting and take dog to the vet.

Bee Sting
Remove stinger and apply soothing lotion or cold compress; give antihistamine in proper dosage.

Bleeding
Apply pressure directly to wound with gauze or towel for five to ten minutes. If wound does not stop bleeding, wrap wound with gauze and adhesive tape.

Bloat/Gastric Torsion
Immediately take the dog to the vet or emergency clinic; phone from car. No time to waste.

Burns
Chemical: Bathe dog with water and pet shampoo. Rinse in saline solution. Apply antibiotic ointment.

Acid: Rinse with water. Apply one part baking soda, two parts water to affected area.

Alkali: Rinse with water. Apply one part vinegar, four parts water to affected area.

Electrical: Apply antibiotic ointment. Seek veterinary assistance immediately.

Choking
If the dog is on the verge of collapsing, wedge a solid object, such as the handle of screwdriver, between molars on one side of mouth to keep mouth open. Pull tongue out. Use long-nosed pliers or fingers to remove foreign object. Do not push the object down the dog's throat. For small or medium dogs, hold dog upside down by hind legs and shake firmly to dislodge foreign object.

Chlorine Ingestion
With clean water, rinse the mouth and eyes. Give dog water to drink; contact the vet.

Constipation
Feed dog 2 tablespoons bran flakes with each meal. Encourage drinking water. Mix 1/4 teaspoon mineral oil in dog's food.

Diarrhea
Withhold food for 12 to 24 hours. Feed dog anti-diarrheal with eyedropper. When feeding resumes, feed one part boiled hamburger, one part plain cooked rice, 1/4- to 3/4 cup four times daily.

Dog Bite
Snip away hair around puncture wound; clean with 3% hydrogen peroxide; apply tincture of iodine. If wound appears deep, take the dog to the vet.

Frostbite
Wrap the dog in a heavy blanket. Warm affected area with a warm bath for ten minutes. Red color to skin will return with circulation; if tissues are pale after 20 minutes, contact the vet.

Use a portable, durable container large enough to contain all items

Heat Stroke
Partially submerge the dog in cold water; if no response within ten minutes, contact the vet.

Hot Spots
Mix 2 packets Domeboro® with 2 cups water. Saturate cloth with mixture and apply to hot spots for 15 to 30 minutes. Apply antibiotic ointment. Repeat every six to eight hours.

Poisonous Plants
Wash affected area with soap and water. Cleanse with alcohol. For foxtail/grass, apply antibiotic ointment.

Rat Poison Ingestion
Induce vomiting. Keep dog calm, maintain dog's normal body temperature (use blanket or heating pad). Get to the vet for antidote.

Shock
Keep the dog calm and warm; call for veterinary assistance.

Snake Bite
If possible, bandage the area and apply pressure. If the area is not conducive to bandaging, use ice to control bleeding. Get immediate help from the vet.

Tick Removal
Apply flea and tick spray directly on tick. Wait one minute. Using tweezers or wearing plastic gloves, apply constant pull while grasping tick's body. Apply antibiotic ointment.

Vomiting
Restrict dog's water intake; offer a few ice cubes. Withhold food for next meal. Contact vet if vomiting persists longer than 24 hours.

DOG OWNER'S FIRST-AID KIT
- ❑ Gauze bandages/swabs
- ❑ Adhesive and non-adhesive bandages
- ❑ Antibiotic powder
- ❑ Antiseptic wash
- ❑ Hydrogen peroxide 3%
- ❑ Antibiotic ointment
- ❑ Lubricating jelly
- ❑ Rectal thermometer
- ❑ Nylon muzzle
- ❑ Scissors and forceps
- ❑ Eyedropper
- ❑ Syringe
- ❑ Anti-bacterial/fungal solution
- ❑ Saline solution
- ❑ Antihistamine
- ❑ Cotton balls
- ❑ Nail clippers
- ❑ Screwdriver/pen knife
- ❑ Flashlight
- ❑ Emergency phone numbers

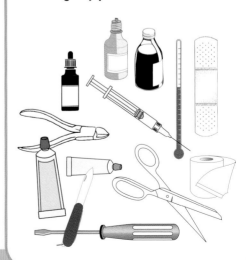

LEONBERGER

Is dog showing in your blood? Are you excited by the idea of gaiting your handsome Leonberger around the ring to the thunderous applause of an enthusiastic audience? Are you certain that your beloved Leonberger is flawless? You are not alone! Every loving owner thinks that his dog has no faults, or too few to mention. No matter how many times an owner reads the breed standard, he cannot find any faults in his aristocratic companion dog. If this sounds like you, and if you are considering entering your Leonberger in a dog show, here are some basic questions to ask yourself:

- Did you purchase a "show-quality" puppy from the breeder?

It looks like Leos and handlers alike are enjoying their time in the ring.

SEAL OF EXCELLENCE
The show ring is the testing ground for a breeder's program. A championship on a dog signifies that three qualified judges have placed their seal of approval on a dog. Only dogs that have earned their championships should be considered for breeding purposes. Striving to improve the breed and reproduce sound, typical examples of the breed, breeders must breed only the best. No breeder breeds only for pet homes; they strive for the top. The goal of every program must be to better the breed, and every responsible breeder wants the prestige of producing Best in Show winners.

- Is your puppy at least six months of age?
- Does the puppy exhibit correct show type for his breed?
- Does your puppy have any disqualifying faults?
- How much time do you have to devote to training, grooming, conditioning and exhibiting your dog?
- Do you understand the rules and regulations of a dog show?

- Do you have time to learn how to show your dog properly?
- Do you have the financial resources to invest in showing your dog?

CLUB CONTACTS

For reliable up-to-date information about registration, dog shows and other canine competitions, contact one of the national clubs by mail or via the Internet.

United Kennel Club
100 E. Kilgore Road, Kalamazoo, MI 49002
www.ukcdogs.com

American Rare Breed Association
9921 Frank Tippett Road
Cheltenham, MD 20623
www.arba.org

International All Breed Canine Association
4742 Liberty Road South, PMB 234
Salem, OR 97302
www.iabcaofamerica@aol.com

Rarities Inc.
1623 Military Road #577
Niagara Falls, NY 14304
www.vaxxine.com/rarities/index.htm

Fédération Cynologique Internationale
14, rue Leopold II, B-6530 Thuin, Belgium
www.fci.be

Canadian Kennel Club
89 Skyway Ave., Suite 100, Etobicoke,
Ontario M9W 6R4 Canada
www.ckc.ca

The Kennel Club
1-5 Clarges St., Piccadilly
London W1Y 8AB, UK
www.the-kennel-club.org.uk

A group of Leonbergers relaxes in the benching area at an outdoor show.

- Will you show the dog yourself or hire a professional handler?
- Do you have a vehicle that can accommodate your weekend trips to the dog shows?

Success in the show ring requires more than a pretty face, a waggy tail and a pocketful of liver. Even though dog shows can be exciting and enjoyable, the sport of conformation makes great demands on the exhibitors and the dogs. Dog showing is a costly and time-consuming hobby, as exhibitors travel to shows all over the US. With the aim of earning championships, exhibitors devote time and money to their dogs' presentation, conditioning and training. Very few novices, even those with good dogs, will find themselves in the winners' circle, though it does happen. Don't be disheartened, though. Every exhibitor began as a novice and worked his way up to the group ring. It's the "working your way

Junior handler in the ring with her Leo. Many top handlers get their start at a young age through the Junior Handling program.

dogs can represent a very considerable investment—over $100,000 has been spent in campaigning some dogs. (The investment can be less, of course, for owners who don't use professional handlers.)

Many owners, on the other hand, enter their "average" Leonbergers in dog shows for the fun and enjoyment of it. Dog showing makes an absorbing hobby, with many rewards for dogs and owners alike. If you're having fun, meeting other people who share your interests and enjoying the overall experience, you likely will catch the "bug." Once the dog-show bug bites, its effects can last a lifetime.

RARE-BREED SHOWING

UNITED KENNEL CLUB

Rare breeds in the United States have many opportunities to compete in both conformation and other events. A glance at the United Kennel Club (UKC) website (www.ukcdogs.com) tells us that the UKC is America's second oldest and second largest all-breed dog registry, attracting around 250,000 registrations each year. Chauncey Z. Bennett founded the UKC in 1898 with an aim to support the "total dog," meaning a dog that possesses quality in physical conformation and performance alike. With that in mind, the UKC sponsors competitive events that emphasize

up" part that you must keep in mind.

Assuming that you have purchased a puppy of the correct type and quality for showing, let's begin to examine the world of showing and what's required to get started. Although the entry fee into a dog show is nominal, there are lots of other hidden costs involved with "finishing" your Leonberger, that is, making him a champion. Things like equipment, travel, training and conditioning all cost money. A more serious campaign will include fees for a professional handler, boarding, cross-country travel and advertising. Top-winning show

SHOW POTENTIAL

How possible is it to predict how your ten-week-old puppy will eventually do in the show ring? Most show dogs reach their prime at around three years of age, when their bodies are physically mature and their coats are in "full bloom." Experienced breeders, having watched countless pups grow into Best of Breed winners, recognize the glowing attributes that spell "show potential." When selecting a puppy for show, it's best to trust the breeder to recommend which puppy will best suit your aspirations. Some breeders recommend starting with a male puppy, which likely will be more "typey" than his female counterpart.

this "total dog" aspect. Along with traditional conformation shows, the UKC's performance events encompass just about every skill that one could imagine in a dog. These performance events include obedience, agility, weight pulls, water races, hunting tests designed for specific types of dog (retrievers, Beagles, curs and feists, etc.) and much more. The website goes on to say, "Essentially, the UKC world of dogs is a working world. That's the way founder Chauncey Bennett designed it, and that's the way it remains today."

What many think of as traditional "dog shows" are more formally known as conformation shows. These are competitive events in which dogs are evaluated based on their conformation to their breed's standard, which is the official written description of the ideal representative of that breed. The standards recognized by the UKC are either adopted from those of Europe's canine registry, the Fédération Cynologique Internationale (FCI), or submitted by the American breed club and then revised and adopted by the UKC. At many shows, handlers will receive verbal "critiques" of their dogs; these critiques may always be requested if not given automatically. This critique details a dog's comparison to the breed standard, and the judge also will explain why he placed each dog as he did.

UKC dog shows may be held for one breed only, several breeds or all breeds. UKC shows are arranged differently from the

Strength and power are essential in the Leonberger, whether or not the dog is used for work. Observing a dog's movement is important in determining whether these elements are present.

two dogs then compete for Best of Winners; the dog who is given this award will go on to compete for Best of Breed. Best of Breed competition includes the Best of Winners and dogs that have earned Champion and Grand Champion titles. Earning Best Male or Best Female, as long as there is competition, is considered a "major."

Once a dog has earned three "majors" and accumulated 100 points, he is considered a UKC champion. What this means is that the dog is now ready to compete for the title of Grand Champion, which is equivalent to an AKC championship. To earn the Grand Champion title, a dog must compete with a minimum of two other dogs who are also

Proud breeder Lynette Hodge and Stormchaser Stole My Heart, the top-winning Leo puppy and overall top-winning Leo in Great Britain for the year 2000.

conformation shows of other organizations. Entries are restricted by age, and you cannot show your dog in a class other than his correct age class. When you compete for championship points, you may enter Puppy (6–12 months), Junior (1–2 years), Senior (2–3 years) or Adult (3 years and older). You may also enter the Breeder/Handler Class, where dogs of all ages compete, but the dog must be handled by his breeder or a member of the breeder's immediate family. The winners of each class compete for Best Male or Best Female. These

EXPRESS YOURSELF

The most intangible of all canine attributes, expression speaks to the character of the breed, attained by the combined features of the head. The shape and balance of the dog's skull, the color and position of the eyes and the size and carriage of the head mingle to produce the correct expression of the breed. A judge may approach a dog and determine instantly whether the dog's face portrays the desired impression for the breed, conveying nobility, intelligence and alertness among other specifics of the breed standard.

CANINE GOOD CITIZEN® PROGRAM

Have you ever considered getting your dog "certified"? The AKC's Canine Good Citizen® Program affords your dog just that opportunity. Your dog shows that he is a well-behaved canine citizen, using the basic training and good manners you have taught him, by taking a series of ten tests that illustrate that he can behave properly at home, in a public place and around other dogs. The tests are administered by participating dog clubs, colleges, 4-H clubs, Scouts and other community groups and are open to all pure-bred (even those breeds not recognized by the AKC) and mixed-breed dogs. Upon passing the ten tests, the suffix CGC is then applied to your dog's name.

The ten tests are: 1. Accepting a friendly stranger; 2. Sitting politely for petting; 3. Appearance and grooming; 4. Walking on a lead; 5. Walking through a group of people; 6. Sit, down and stay on command; 7. Coming when called; 8. Meeting another dog; 9. Calm reaction to distractions; 10. Separation from owner.

prestigious one. Once a dog has earned the Grand Champion title, he can continue to compete for Top Ten, but there are no further titles to earn. "Top Ten" refers to the ten dogs in each breed that have won the most points in a given year. These dogs compete in a Top Ten invitational competition annually.

The breeds recognized by the UKC are divided into groups. The Leonberger competes in the Guardian Group, which consists of dogs of similar utility and/or heritage. Depending on the show-giving club, group competition may or may not be offered. A group must have a minimum of five breeds entered in order for group competition to take place. If

champions. The dog must win this class, called the Champion of Champions class, five times under three different judges. In rare breeds, it is difficult to assemble a class of champions, so the UKC Grand Champion title is truly a

No stone is left unturned as all aspects of the dog are given a hands-on evaluation. Here the judge inspects the Leo's feet.

DRESS THE PART

It's a dog show, so don't forget your costume. Even though the show is about the dog, you also must play your role well. You have been cast as the "dog handler" and you must smartly dress the part. Solid colors make a nice complement to the dog's coat, but choose colors that contrast. You don't want to be wearing a solid color that blends mostly or entirely with the major or only color of your dog. Whether the show is indoors or out, you still must dress properly. You want the judge to perceive you as being professional, so polish, polish, polish! And don't forget to wear sensible shoes; remember, you have to gait around the ring with your dog.

group competition is offered, Best in Show consists of the group winners. If there is no group competition, then all Best of Breed dogs go into the ring at the same time to compete for Best in Show. This can be a large number of dogs and thus can be very interesting, to say the least!

Aside from the variations already presented, UKC shows differ from other dog shows in one very significant way: no professional handlers are allowed to show dogs, except for those dogs they own themselves. UKC shows create an atmosphere that is owner-friendly, relaxed and genuinely fun. Bait in the ring is allowed at the discretion of the judge, but throwing the bait, dropping it on the floor or other "handler tricks" will get an owner excused from the ring in a big hurry.

In addition to dog shows, the UKC offers many, many more venues for dogs and their owners, in keeping with its mission of promoting the "total dog." UKC obedience events test the training of dogs as they perform a series of prescribed exercises at the commands of their handlers. There are several levels of competition, ranging from basic commands such as "sit," "come" and "heel," to advanced exercises like scent discrimination and directed retrieves over jumps, based on the dog's level of

OPPORTUNITIES FOR JUNIORS

For budding dog handlers, as young as 2 years old and through 18 years old, the UKC's Total Junior Program is an excellent training ground for the next generation of dog professionals. Owning and caring for a dog are wonderful methods of teaching children responsibility, and the Total Junior Program builds upon that foundation. Juniors learn by grooming, training and handling their dogs, and the quality of the junior handler's presentation of the dog (and of himself) is evaluated by a licensed judge. More than just conformation showing, this program puts the emphasis on "total," with divisions for juniors offered in showmanship, agility, obedience and weight-pulling classes to encourage all-around participation and achievement in the canine sport. Aside from the competitive aspect, emphasis is placed on proper treatment of the dogs as well as good sportsmanship.

Competition for juniors is divided into four age categories: Pee-Wee (ages 2 to under 4); Sub-Junior (ages 4 to under 8); Junior (ages 8 to under 13); and Senior (ages 13 to under 19). Showmanship classes for the Junior and Senior age groups are further divided into Novice and Open. Juniors can compete with any UKC-registered dog that is at least six months of age.

In addition to awards and points given out on show days, juniors can be eligible for other special awards. These include the Total Junior award, recognizing achievement in two or more areas of the sport; the Top Ten competition, a national competition among the top ten juniors in each of the four areas of competition; the Junior Service award, recognizing a junior's involvement in promoting responsible breeding, training and ownership of dogs; and the Junior Showmanship award; a peer-selected honor.

Regardless of the area of competition, dog and handler must work as a team, follow the judge's directions and display poise, confidence and consideration for other competitors. Those licensed to judge junior competition have a wonderful opportunity to teach and mold the future of the dog sport. Judges are encouraged to officiate in a manner that will help young people to continue to learn, to improve their handling skills and to increase their knowledge of show procedure and regulations.

accomplishment. The classes are further delineated by the experience of the handler.

UKC obedience differs from AKC obedience in many respects. Even at the most basic levels, the dogs are expected to "honor" other dogs who are working. In other words, the "honoring" dog must be placed in a down/stay while his owner leaves the ring and moves out of sight. The dog must remain in the down/stay position while the working dog

Shows can be enjoyable social events for everyone—owners, handlers, spectators and Leonbergers!

OTHER RARE-BREED ORGANIZATIONS

In addition to the United Kennel Club, there are several other organizations that offer registration and competitive events. The availability of these events depends on geography. The IABCA (International All Breed Canine Association of America) holds conformation shows under FCI rules. This club offers both American and international judges at all of their shows. Most of their events are held in the western US, but now also are offered in both the Midwest and Florida.

goes through the heeling exercises.

Agility events are fast-paced exercises in which the handler directs his dog through a course involving tunnels, sway bridges, jumps and other obstacles in a race against the clock. The dogs are scored according to the manner in which they negotiate the obstacles and the time elapsed to complete the course. UKC agility is very similar to AKC agility; clubs often will offer both AKC and UKC agility events (not on the same day).

As with UKC shows, IABCA shows divide dogs by age. Dogs are considered "puppies" up to 18 months of age for large breeds and up to 15 months of age for smaller breeds. You cannot enter your dog in any class except the appropriate class for his age. After puppyhood, you can enter your dog in the adult class. Once your dog has earned his championship,

The collapsed tunnel seems to present only a minor challenge to this Leo, who tackles the obstacle "head on."

he goes on to compete for various ranks of champion, of which there are too many to enumerate here. There are fun classes as well, one of which is "Best Rare Breed in Show." This class is only offered on the Sunday of a show weekend, and only those dogs earning the highest award possible in their classes may enter (Best Puppy, Best of Breed).

In order for a dog to earn a championship, he must receive three V-1 ratings. Each dog is given a written critique during the class. The judge will ask the

SO MUCH TO DO!

The bottom line is this: there is so much to do with your dog that it can be hard to decide which event to try! Just as we have to choose what to do with our weekends, so do the dogs. Whatever you choose to do with your dog, it will take training, dedication and a willingness to work with your dog to achieve a common goal, a partnership between you and your dog. There is nothing more pleasing than to watch a handler and dog performing at a high level, whether it is the show ring or in a performance event. There is something for everyone and every dog in the world of dog "showing." Dog showing should really be called "competing with your dog." You are not restricted to the traditional "dog show" and may find that your "show dog" excels in other areas as well or instead.

handler to stand near the judges' table and will either make notes or dictate to the ring steward as he compares your dog to the standard. A handler can listen while the judge does this and often the judge will ask questions, especially of handlers showing rare-breed dogs. It is a very interesting and educational procedure, to say the least. Rare breeds can earn a championship without competing against other dogs, because the dog is always competing against the breed standard. There are times when no dog in a breed receives a V-1 if none is of sufficient quality to warrant such a rating.

Another organization, the American Rare Breed Association (ARBA), holds shows across the country, although not in great numbers. In ARBA competition, as in IABCA competition, a dog is able to win points and earn his championship by showing against the standard, not necessarily against other dogs. The Cherry Blossom show, held annually in Washington, DC each spring, draws a handsome entry.

A show-giving group called Rarities Inc. also has arrived on the scene in the United States and Canada. This group is dedicated to the support of ancient and rare breeds. To obtain a championship, a dog requires 15 points. Of these 15 points, the dog must have attained two "majors" of at least

TEN GROUPS

The FCI is divided into ten groups that classify the breeds by traditional functions. The official breed list indicates whether or not the breed requires a Working Trial in order to earn the CACIB title. (The Leonberger is in Group 2 and does not require a Working Trial.)

Group 1: Sheepdogs and Cattledogs (except Swiss Cattledogs)

Group 2: Pinschers and Schnauzers, Molossians, Swiss Mountain dogs and Swiss Cattledogs

Group 3: Terriers

Group 4: Dachshunds

Group 5: Spitz- and Primitive-type dogs

Group 6: Scenthounds and Related Breeds

Group 7: Pointing dogs

Group 8: Retrievers, Flushing dogs and Water dogs

Group 9: Companion and Toy dogs

Group 10: Sighthounds

three points under two different judges; further, the total of 15 points must have been obtained under 3 different judges. Shows with double points awarded count toward both the American and Canadian championship. To earn the International Championship, the dog must win both the American and Canadian championships. The Grand Champion title is earned by defeating 15 other Rarities or FCI champions. Grand Champions (not pending Grand Champions) may compete for the title Supreme Grand Champion, which is earned by defeating 15 other Rarities Grand Champions. In Rarities shows, as in UKC shows, a dog must defeat other dogs in order to earn a championship. One of the unique things about Rarities, Inc. is that all Working Group breeds must also pass a temperament test.

FÉDÉRATION CYNOLOGIQUE INTERNATIONALE

The Fédération Cynologique Internationale (FCI) aims to encourage and promote the breeding and use of pure-bred dogs that properly represent their breed standards and are capable of working in their bred-for capacities, as well as to protect the breeding and keeping of dogs around the world and to support the open exchange of dogs and information between member countries. Founded on May 22, 1911, the FCI today operates around the world in 79 member countries, divided into five regional groups, which include Europe, the Americas and the Caribbean, Asia, Africa and Oceania and Australia. When the organization was established it included only five countries: Germany, Austria, France, Netherlands and Belgium. The Société Royale Saint-Hubert of

Belgium deserves credit for recreating the organization in 1921 after it disappeared during World War I.

Recognizing over 330 breeds, nearly twice the number of any other registry, the FCI considers each breed as the "property" of its native country and recognizes the breed standard of the country of origin. All 79 member countries conduct both International Shows and Working/Hunting Trials. National shows are held, though these shows are governed by the rules of the member country and not the FCI.

FCI conformation shows are sometimes called "beauty shows" and differ in many respects from the shows of other kennel clubs. For example, each dog is critiqued by the judge in writing, and these

For a large dog, the Leo proves to be surprisingly agile as it easily clears the bar jump in an agility trial.

The judge reviews the line-up of Leos as he mentally compares each one to the breed standard.

other kennel clubs and also demands that the judge be able to "document" his decision for placing the dog first or last. The judges assign the following qualifications to dogs: Excellent (close to ideal, excellent condition, good balance and superior presentation); Very Good (typical of breed and well-balanced, with a few minor faults); Good (most breed characteristics with faults), Sufficient or Satisfactory (corresponds to breed but not typical), Disqualified (atypical with serious faults) and Cannot Be Judged (uncontrolled in ring).

"judge's reports" are available to the exhibitor. The judge must detail his evaluation and designate a grade to the dog, based entirely on conformation to the standard. This process is far more time-consuming than that of

The FCI's most prestigious

Leonbergers stacked in the ring at a show, awaiting their turns with the judge.

ON THE MOVE

The truest test of a dog's proper structure is his gait, the way the dog moves. That the dog moves smoothly and effortlessly indicates to the judge that the dog's structure is well made. From the four-beat gallop, the fastest of canine gaits, to the high-lifting hackney gait, each breed varies in its correct gait; not every breed is expected to move in the same way. Each breed standard defines the correct gait for its breed and often identifies movement faults, such as toeing in, side-winding, over-reaching or crossing over.

shows are the all-breed shows, such as the World Dog Show, followed by the Sections show, like the European Dog Show, and then the International Championship Shows. National shows can be all-breed shows, Group Championship Shows, Breed or Specialty Shows, Open Shows, Club Shows and Young Dog Shows. At all of these shows, dogs can earn World or European Championship titles or the CACIB certificate. The *Certificat d'Aptitude au Championnat International de Beauté* is the International Certificate won by dogs; the National Certificate is known as the *Certificat d'Aptitude au Championnat National de Beauté* (CAC). The judge awards the CACIB Certificate to a superior dog in the Open, Working or Champion Class. A dog that has won four CACIBs (without Working or Hunting Trial) is designated an International Beauty Champion, provided that the certificates were won in three different countries, one of which must be the country of residence or origin. The title National Beauty Champion is awarded to a dog who has earned two, three or four CACs, depending on the country. The titles International Champion and National Champion are reserved only for those breeds that must undergo Working or Hunting Trials.

The following classes are offered at FCI shows: Puppy Class (6–9 months of age), Junior Class (9–18 months of age), Intermediate Class (15–24 months of age), Open Class, Working Class and Champion Class (these latter three, all 15 months of age and over); Veterans Class (eight years of age and over).

For more information about the FCI, show schedules and rules and regulations, you can visit the website at www.fci.be. The FCI also publishes the *Trimestrial Magazine* in four languages (French, English, German and Spanish). Contact Stratego, Muhlenweg 4, 7221 Marz, Austria for information about the magazine.

INDEX

Page numbers in **boldface** indicate illustrations.

Abe 28
Activities 26, 107-109, 151
Addison's disease 125
Adenovirus 122
Adult
—adoption 86
—Class 145
—diet 67-68
—health 115
—training 84, 86
Affection 19
After-sale support 42
Aggression 19, 20, 60, 87, 88, 124
Agility 24, 108-109, 149
Aging 115, 117
Allergies 125
Alpha role 96
American Heartworm Society 139
American Kennel Club 16, 30, 143, 147
—Companion Animal Recovery 80
American Rare Breed Association 143, 152
Anal sacs 78
Ancylostoma braziliense 135
Ancylostoma caninum **125, 128**
Anecdotes 27-28
Antifreeze 54, 55, 119
Antoinette, Marie 15
Appetite loss 71, 115, 119
Ascarid **134, 135**
Ascaris lumbricoides **134**
Attention 97-98, 103
—need for 25, 38
Austria 14-15
Backpacking 108
Bait 148
Ballard, Wendy 82
Barney 26
Bathing 77
Bedding 47, 59, 92
Bennett, Chauncey Z. 144-145
Bernese Mountain Dogs 107
Best Female 146
Best in Show 143, 147
Best Male 146
Best of Breed 146
Best of Winners 146
Best Rare Breed in Show 150
Bismarck 26
Black Forest 15
Bloat 68, 69-70, 119, 140
Boarding 82-83
Body language 22, 87, 94, 100
Body temperature 111
Bones 48
Bordetella bronchiseptica 124
Bordetella parainfluenza 122
Borrelia burgdorfei 122
Borreliosis 124
Bowls 45
Breed clubs 12, 39, 145
—events 15, 107
Breeder 30, 39, 41-44, 111
Breeder/Handler Class 146
Breeding 143

Britain 16
Brown, Melanie 15
Bruno 21
Brushing 72
CAC 155
CACIB 152, 155
Campbell, Kerry 15
Canadian Kennel Club 143
Cancer 116, 124
Canine cough 122
Canine development schedule 90
Canine Eye Registration Foundation 41, 125
Canine Good Citizen® program 147
Canis domesticus 15
Canis lupus 15
Car travel 58, 81-82
Carting 14, 107
Cat 62
Cataracts 79, 125
Champion 143, 146
Champion of Champions class 146
Cherry Blossom show 152
Chew toys 48-50, 63, 91, 93
Chewing 47, 49, 61, 88
Cheyletiella mite **131**
Chiggers 133
Children 19, 21-22, 23, 58, 60, 62, 64, 87, 88
Classes at shows 145
—FCI 155
Coat 24
—maintenance 71
—top coat 71
—undercoat 71
Cognitive dysfunction 117
Collar 50-52, 80, 88, 97
Combing 72
Come 102-103
Commands 64, 99
—obedience 98-105
—potty 91
—practicing 99, 101
Commitment of ownership 42
Comtois, Alida 17
Conformation 153
—classes at 145
—for rare breeds 143
—showing 144
Consistency 54, 61, 63, 95, 98, 109
Contract 41
Core vaccines 123
Coronavirus 122, 124
Correction 97
Crate 46, 58-59, 65,
—pads 47
—training 87-95
Critique 145, 151, 154
Crufts 16
Crying 59, 64, 92
Ctenocephalides canis **126**
Dangers in the home 52, 54
Decher, Mary & Reiner 15
DEET 133
Delta Society 22

Demodectic mange 42
Demodex mite **133**
Demodicosis 132-133
Dental care 72, 115, 117, 119, 125
Deutscher Klub für Leonberger Hunde e.V. 12, 17
Devotion 22
Diet 66
—adult 67-68
—homemade 67
—making changes 68
—puppy 66-67
—sheet 41, 66
Dilated cardiomyopathy 125
Disabled 23
Dipylidium caninum 136 138
Dirofilaria immitis 137, **138**, 139
Discipline 96
Distemper 122, 123
Documentation with puppy 42
Dog club 39
Dog fight 88
Dog flea 126
Dog food 66-67
DogGone™ newsletter 82
Dominance 99
Down 63, 93, 100
Down/stay 102
Draft-dog trials 107
Drop it 87
Ear
—care 72, 75
—mite 75, 131-132
Echinococcus multilocularis 137
Ectropion 125
Edward VII 28
Elbow dysplasia 41, 125
Elizabeth, Empress of Austria 14
Elsa 28
Emergency care 119, 140-141
Entropion 125
Ersteen 107
Essig, Heinrich 9-12, 14, 15, 30, 32
Estrus 20, 113, 124
European Dog Show 155
Exercise 68, 70-71
—pen 91
Expenses 38, 47
External parasites 126-133
Eye care 78-79
Eye health 41
Eye problems 125
Family meeting the puppy 58
Fear period 60-61
Fédération Cynologique Internationale 17, 30, 143, 145, 153-155
—breed standard 31-37
Feeding 66-70
Fenced yard 54, 55, 88
Fertilizers 54, 55
Finding lost dog 79
Fiona 15
First aid 119, 140-141
First night in new home 59
First-time owner 19
Fleas **126**, 127, **128**
Flyball 28, 71, 107

Food 68, 92
—allergies 125
—bowls 45
—loss of interest in 71, 115, 119
—rewards 64, 85, 96, 98, 106
—toxic to dogs 55, 67
Gait 155
Gastric torsion 68, 69-70, 119, 140
Genetic testing 113
Gentle Giant 19
Germany 9-14, 15, 30
Giardia 122
Gineste, Mlle. de 15
Give it 87
Glaucoma 125
Golden Sunset 16
Gower, Mr. D. T. 16
Grand Champion 146, 152
Grass
—eating 72
Gray wolf 15
Great Dane 9, **10**
Great Pyrenees 9, 10, **11**
Grooming 72-79
Group competition 147
Grosslight, Susan 17
Guide dogs for the blind 23
Gum disease 115
Handler 143, 146, 148
—junior 149
Harvey 28
Health 54, 125
—adult 115
—benefits of dog ownership 20
—insurance for pets 121
—journal 56
—problems 119-125
—puppy 38, 56, 113
—senior dog 117
—signs of problems 119
Heart problems 117, 125
Heartworm 115, 117, 137, **138, 139**
Heat cycles 20, 113, 124
Heel 103-105
Height 25
Hepatitis 122, 123
Hereditary concerns 41, 78, 116, 118, 125
Heterodoxus spiniger **132**
Hip dysplasia 41, 118
HomeAgain™ Companion Animal Retrieval System 80
Homemade toys 50
Hookworm **135, 138**
Hot spot 125
Hot-weather problems 71
House-training 46, 59, 87-95
—puppy needs 89
—schedule 94-95
Hunting trial 153
Hypothyroidism 125
Identification 79-81
Infectious diseases 121-123
Inherited polyneuropathy 125
Insurance 121
Intelligence 22-23
Internal parasites 134-139

International All Breed Canine Association of America 143, 150
International Beauty Champion 155
International Certificate 155
International Champion 152, 155
International Championship Show 155
International Leonberger Club 12
Internationale Union für Leonberger Hunde 12, 15, 17
Ixodes dammini **129-130**
Judges 143
—interpretation 31
—report 153
Jumping up 63, 93
Junior Class 145
Junior handling 149
Junior diet 67
Junior program 149
Kaufmann, Sylvia & Manfred 15
Kennel Club, The 143
Kennel von Alpensee 17
Kennel von Jagen 17
Kidney problems 117, 125
Kienzle, Albert 12
Kiseirdi Nora 15, 14, **17, 32**
Klub für Leonberger Hunde 12
Landseer Newfoundland 10, **13**
Laryngeal paralysis 117
Leash 28, 52, 53, 92, 97
—pulling on 105
Lehmann, Otto 12
Lens luxation 125
Leo Letter 16
Leonberg 9, 12, 15
Leonberger Club of America 15-17, 39, 125
Leonberger Club of Heidelberg 12
Leonberger Health Foundation 125
Leonberger (Hunde) Club 12
Leptospirosis 122, 124
Lethargy 119
Lifespan 115
Liver problems 125
Litter box 60
Lost dog 80
Louse **132**
Lyme disease 122, 124
Majors 146, 152
Mammary cancer 124
Mange 42
Maturity 19, 22
Maximilian, Emperor 14
Metternich family 14
Microchip 79-80
Mikado of Japan 14
Missing teeth 125
Mites 42, 75, **131, 132, 133**
Mosquitoes 133, 137, 139
Mounting 124
Munich Oktoberfest 11
Nail clipping 75
Name 99, 103
National Beauty Champion 155
National Certificate 155
National Champion 155
Neutering 56, 115, 123-124

Newfoundland 9, 10, 13, 23, 71, 109
Nipping 61, 64
Non-core vaccines 124
Northern and Southern California Leonberger Clubs 16
Northwest Leonberger Club 16
Obedience 101
—classes 106
—events 148
—trials 107
Obesity 67
Off 64, 93
Okay 88, 100, 103, 105
Origins 9
Orthopedic Foundation for Animals 41, 125
Osteochondrosis dissecans 125
Other dogs 124
Other pets 60, 87
Otodectes cynotis 131
Outdoors 24, 54
Ovariohysterectomy 113, 124
Ownership 43-44
—considerations 38-39
—expenses of 47
—health benefits of 20
—suitability 19
Pack animals 15, 84, 95-97
Paper-training 88, 94
Paperwork 41
Parainfluenza 124
Parasite 42
—control 115
—external 126-133
—internal 134-139
Parent, Yves 15
Parvovirus 122, 123
Patience 86, 98
Pedigree 42, 44
Perianal fistulas 78
Persistant pupillary membrane 125
Personality 19-28
Peters, Brian 15
Pet Partners Program 22
Pet therapy 22, 23
Plants 52, 55, 119
Playtime 87, 102
Pluival, Marquis de 15
Poisons 52, 54, 55, 67, 119
Polyneuropathy 125
Positive reinforcement 58, 96, 99, 109
Practicing 101
—commands 99
Praise 85, 96, 98, 106
Preventive care 111, 115, 117
Proglottid **137**
Progressive retinal atrophy 125
Prostate problems 124
Protective nature 19, 22
Protein 66, 70
Pulling on leash 105
Punishment 65, 96-97
Puppy
—behavior 38
—common problems 61
—conformation 42
—diet 66
—establishing leadership 85
—exercise 70

—first car ride 58
—first night in new home 59
—health 38, 42, 56, 113
—kindergarten training class 98
—meeting the family 58
—personality 43, 113
—selection 38-44, 86, 111
—show potential 142-143, 145
—socialization 59
—supplies for 44-52
—teething 49, 62
—training 84, 98
Puppy Class 145
Puppy-proofing 46, 52
Pure-bred dogs 11, 30
Pyotraumatic dermatitis 125
Rabies 122, 123
Rare breed 144
—organizations 150
Rarities Inc. 143, 152
Rawhide 49
Registry 16
Rewards 64, 85, 96, 98, 106
—food 96
Rhabditis **138**
Roaming 124
Rocky Mountain Leonberger Club 16
Rope toys 49
Roundworm **134**, 135, **138**
Routine 61, 95
Safety 46, 48, 52, 55, 81, 88, 91, 93, 102
—in car 81-82
—outdoors 54-55
St. Bernard 9, **10**, 11-12, 23
—Hospice 10
Sales contract 42
Sarcoptes scabiei **131**
Scabies 131
Scent attraction 94
Scenting 21
Schedule 61, 94-95
Search and rescue 12, 23
Senior Class 145
Senior dog 115
—health 117
Sense of smell 21
Sex-related differences 19-20
Shedding 71
Shows
—costs of 143
—potential 145
—quality 142, 143
Sit 99
Sit/stay 101
Size 25, 38, 109
Skin conditions 125
Socialization 19, 59-61, 98, 113
Société Royale Saint-Hubert 153
Soft toys 49
Spaying 56, 113, 115, 123-124
Standard 30, 145
Stay 101, 105
Stephanie, Princess of Monaco 26
Stray dog 80
Stress 97
Supervision 62, 93
Supplements 67
Supreme Grand Champion 152
Surgery 124
Swimming 23

Switzerland 24107
Taenia pisiformis **137**
Tapeworm 136, **137, 138**
Tattooing 80
Teeth 72, 115, 119, 125
Teething 38, 49, 62
Temperament 19-28, 41, 43
—evaluation 113
Temperature
—taking your dog's 111
Testicular cancer 124
Therapy dogs 22-23
Tick-borne diseases 129
Ticks 122, **129-130**
Timing 94, 96, 98, 103
Tooth cleaning 72
Top ten 147
Torsion 68
Toxascaris leonine 134
Toxins 52, 54, 55, 67, 119
Toxocara canis **134**
Toys 48-50, 63, 87, 91, 93
Tracheobronchitis 122
Training 27, 54, 64
—commands 98-105
—consistency in 63, 109
—importance of timing 94, 103
—principles 84, 86, 98
Travel 46, 58
Treats 58, 64, 85, 96, 98
—weaning off in training 106
Trichuris sp. **136**
Trimestrial Magazine 155
Trimming 72
Type 142-143
Umberto, King of Italy 14
Umbilical hernias 42
Underweight 70
United Kennel Club 143-150
United States 15-17
Urinary tract problems 113
Urine marking 124
V-1 ratings 151
Vaccinations 56, 61, 115, 121-123
Veterinarian 39, 48-49, 54, 56, 88, 113, 115, 117, 119-121
Veterinary insurance 121
Veterinary specialties 120
Visiting the litter 41, 43
Vitimins 67
Von Baden, Grand Duke Friedrich 26
Von Schutmuth, Professor 12
Wagner, Robert 26
Walking 28, 70
Water 59, 68, 69, 70, 91
—affinity for 23-24, 28, 39
—bowls 24, 45
—excessive intake 119
Water trials 71, 109
Weather 24
Weigelschmidt, Hans 12
Weight 67
West Nile virus 133
Whining 59, 64, 92
Whipworm **136**
Wolf 15
Working trials 107, 153
World Dog Show 154
World Wars 12, 153
Worm control 136
Yard 54, 55, 88
Zieher, Waltraud 15

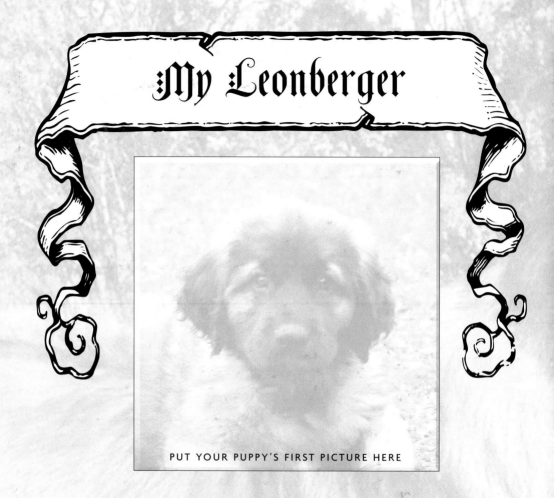

My Leonberger

PUT YOUR PUPPY'S FIRST PICTURE HERE

Dog's Name _____

Date _____ Photographer _____